FRANCE

Welcome to France

F. George Kay

Collins
Glasgow and London

Cover photographs
Van Phillips

Photographs
J Allan Cash Ltd
pp. 28, 29, 32, 36 (mid l., bottom rt), 40, 60, 61,
67 (bottom l.), 70 (bottom l. and rt), 75, 77, 79, 82
(top rt), 83, 84, 91 (mid l., bottom rt), 93 (mid rt),
98, 101, 102, 107, 114 (bottom rt), 116, 121, 123,
124 (bottom l., top rt, bottom rt)

Mike Andrews
pp. 92/3 (centre)

Pictor
pp. 51, 109, 114 (top l.)

Picturepoint Ltd
pp. 36 (top rt), 95

Robert Harding Associates
pp. 53, 88 (top rt)

Ronald Sheridan
pp. 59, 81, 82 (mid l., bottom rt), 88 (mid l.,
bottom rt), 89, 92 (mid l.)

Van Phillips
pp. 33 (top l., mid rt), 67 (top l., top rt, bottom rt)

Zefa
pp. 9, 49, 57, 99, 106, 110

Regional maps
Mike Shand

Town plans
M and R Piggott

Illustrations
Barry Rowe

First published 1980
Revised edition published 1985
Copyright © F. George Kay 1980
Published by William Collins Sons and Company Limited
Printed in Great Britain
ISBN 0 00 447394 9

HOW TO USE THIS BOOK

The contents page of this book shows how the country is divided up into tourist regions. The book is in two sections; general information and gazetteer. The latter is arranged in the tourist regions with an introduction and a regional map (detail below left). There are also plans of the main towns (detail below right). All the towns and villages in the gazetteer are shown on the regional maps. Places to visit and leisure facilities available in each region and town are indicated by symbols. Main roads, railways, ferries and airports are shown on the maps and plans.

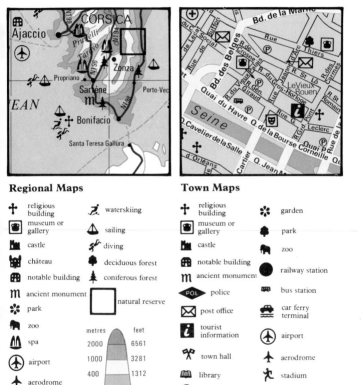

Regional Maps

†	religious building	🎿	waterskiing
🖼	museum or gallery	⛵	sailing
🏰	castle	🤿	diving
🏰	château	🌳	deciduous forest
🏛	notable building	🌲	coniferous forest
m	ancient monument		natural reserve
❀	park		
🐘	zoo	metres / feet	
♒	spa	2000 / 6561	
✈	airport	1000 / 3281	
		400 / 1312	
✈	aerodrome	200 / 656	
▲	mountaineering	0 / 0	
🕳	caving		
🎿	skiing		

Scale 1:2,500,000

0   20   40   60   80 kms

0   10   20   30   40   50 miles

Town Maps

†	religious building	❀	garden
🖼	museum or gallery	♠	park
🏰	castle	🐘	zoo
🏛	notable building		railway station
m	ancient monument		
POL	police	🚌	bus station
✉	post office	🚢	car ferry terminal
i	tourist information	✈	airport
⚒	town hall	✈	aerodrome
📖	library	🏃	stadium
✛	hospital	🏊	swimming pool
🎭	theatre	🏇	racecourse
🎰	casino	tennis courts	
🏪	market	⚓	harbour
⛺	youth hostel	🏖	beach

Every effort has been made to give you an up-to-date text but changes are constantly occurring and we will be grateful for any information about changes you may notice while travelling.

CONTENTS

Town Plans

Regions and Departments

1 Brittany and Normandy
14 Calvados
22 Côtes-du-Nord
27 Eure
29 Finistère
35 Ille-et-Vilaine
50 Manche
44 Loire-Atlantique
61 Orne
76 Seine-Maritime
56 Morbihan

2 Northern France
02 Aisne
59 Nord
60 Oise
62 Pas-de-Calais
80 Somme

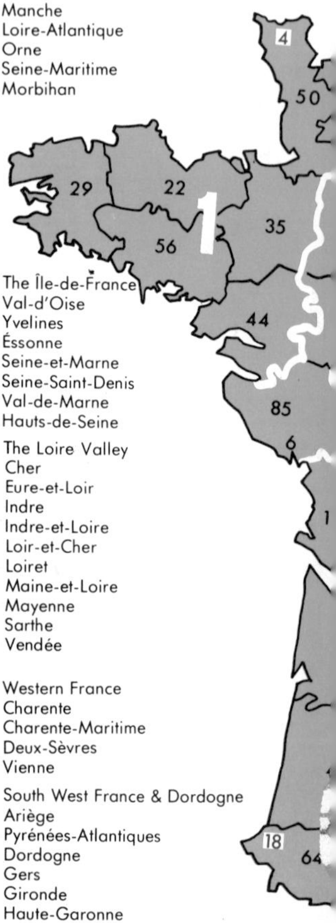

3 The Île-de-France
95 Val-d'Oise
78 Yvelines
91 Éssonne
77 Seine-et-Marne
93 Seine-Saint-Denis
94 Val-de-Marne
92 Hauts-de-Seine

4 The Loire Valley
18 Cher
28 Eure-et-Loir
36 Indre
37 Indre-et-Loire
41 Loir-et-Cher
45 Loiret
49 Maine-et-Loire
53 Mayenne
72 Sarthe
85 Vendée

6 Western France
16 Charente
17 Charente-Maritime
79 Deux-Sèvres
84 Vienne

7 South West France & Dordogne
09 Ariège
64 Pyrénées-Atlantiques
24 Dordogne
32 Gers
33 Gironde
31 Haute-Garonne
65 Hautes-Pyrénées
40 Landes
47 Lot-et-Garonne
81 Tarn
82 Tarn-et-Garonne

8 Central France
03 Allier
07 Ardèche
12 Aveyron
15 Cantal
19 Corrèze
23 Creuse
43 Haute-Loire
87 Haute-Vienne
42 Loire
46 Lot
48 Lozère
63 Puy-de-Dôme

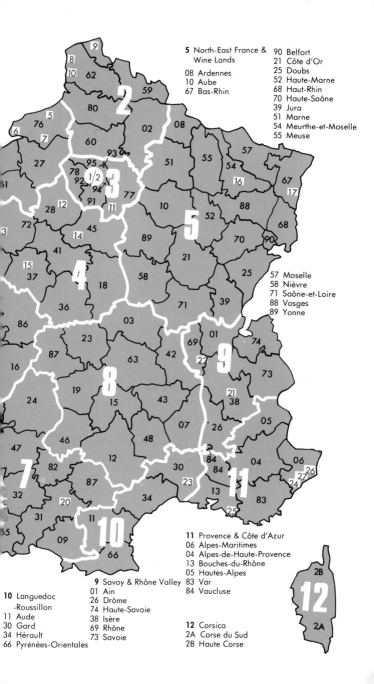

5 North-East France & Wine Lands

08 Ardennes
10 Aube
67 Bas-Rhin

90 Belfort
21 Côte d'Or
25 Doubs
52 Haute-Marne
68 Haut-Rhin
70 Haute-Saône
39 Jura
51 Marne
54 Meurthe-et-Moselle
55 Meuse

57 Moselle
58 Nièvre
71 Saône-et-Loire
88 Vosges
89 Yonne

11 Provence & Côte d'Azur
06 Alpes-Maritimes
04 Alpes-de-Haute-Provence
13 Bouches-du-Rhône
05 Hautes-Alpes
83 Var
84 Vaucluse

12 Corsica
2A Corse du Sud
2B Haute Corse

10 Languedoc
-Roussillon
11 Aude
30 Gard
34 Hérault
66 Pyrénées-Orientales

9 Savoy & Rhône Valley
01 Ain
26 Drôme
74 Haute-Savoie
38 Isère
69 Rhône
73 Savoie

FRANCE

France is a land of great variety of climate and terrain. For its size – 55 million hectares/213,000 sq mi – the contrasts are remarkable. In the south some areas are semitropical, with lemons, oranges, rice and even a few bananas thriving. Within an hour's journey by car or train, the slopes of Europe's highest mountain (Mont Blanc, 4807m/15,700ft) offer skiing even in midsummer. On the high plateau of the Massif Central there are major variations in seasonal temperatures, with cold winters and dry, hot summers. On the west coast and in Brittany the Atlantic keeps the climate moist and cool. Around Paris and in the north the weather is comparable to that of southern England, but with a lower rainfall.

France is one of the most fertile countries on earth. This is due to the ring of lowlands around the high central mass, and to the Alps and Pyrenees which contribute to the natural irrigation. No area is very far from a large river. The Loire, Rhône, Garonne, Seine and Rhine fertilize immense areas as well as contribute to the country's transport system and electricity supplies.

For the purposes of administration the country is divided into 24 regions (including the districts of Paris and Corsica), and each is subdivided into departments (mentioned after the name of each place in the Gazetteer). Under the Fifth Republic, Parliament consists of two Houses: the National Assembly and the Senate. The President is elected for a term of seven years by direct universal suffrage. The Prime Minister is appointed by the President, who also confirms the Cabinet appointments recommended by the Prime Minister.

The population totals more than 53 million. The French are a highly individualistic people, which is the reason why political controversy is never far from a Frenchman's mind. An objective interest in the political situation on the part of the tourist can greatly add to the interest of the visit, though it should be said that ignorant criticism will not be accepted. Nor should it be considered that a view acceptable in Paris will be echoed elsewhere. A Frenchman is a national patriot but he is also parochial in his attitudes.

Prone to live within his own locality, the Frenchman has long been blessed with easy communication with his neighbours.

Ever since Napoleon built the French road system, it has been claimed as the most comprehensive in the world. There are 1½ million km/930,000 mi of roads and more than 5000km/3200mi of autoroutes (most with tolls for stages).

'All roads lead to Paris' is true so far as the original strategy of Napoleon's plan is concerned. They enabled him to move troops quickly and easily to the land frontiers and the main ports. But an equal number criss-cross the country to connect every important provincial town and to serve the natural areas into which France can be divided.

For the purpose of providing a survey of the regions of interest to tourists the areas may be grouped as follows: the city of **Paris**; the region surrounding the capital, historically known as the **Île-de-France**, made up of seven departments, and for administrative purposes called the **Région Parisienne**; the ancient provinces of **Brittany** and **Normandy** on the northwest coast; **Northern France**, including the departments of Nord and Somme; the **Loire Valley**; **North-East France and the Wine Lands** covering the provinces of Burgundy, Champagne-Ardenne, Lorraine and Alsace; **Western France**, bordering the Atlantic Ocean; **South-West France and the Dordogne**, including the province of Aquitaine and the slopes of the Pyrenees; **Central France**; **Savoy and the Rhône Valley** stretching to the mountains and the Rhine; **Languedoc-Roussillon**, the area newly developed on the coast between the Spanish border and Marseille; **Provence and the Côte d'Azur**, the world's most famous region of coastal resorts and mountains; and finally **Corsica**, the island which is administratively part of Metropolitan France.

No visitor restricted to two or three weeks should attempt to see the whole country; the surfeit of hurried sightseeing and thousands of miles of travel will merely bewilder; nor, with the wealth of sights in every area, should he be content

to stay in one place. The happy medium of choosing a centre and enjoying a series of half-day or day-long visits is ideal.

The traditional view of France is that of a capital city devoted to the arts, profiting from bizarre amusements for foreigners, prone to revolution; and beyond it a vast countryside inhabited only by a peasant class, old-fashioned, sentimental and slow-moving.

If it was ever true, it certainly is not now. France is emerging from her second Renaissance. In 1973 she became third largest exporting nation on earth – among the first half dozen in the production of iron ore and steel, and of automobile manufacture. Modern achievements include the world's first solar furnace at Mont-Louis and a major tide-harnessing project above St-Malo.

France's vital industry, agriculture, is indirectly the reason why France is such a beautiful country to visit. This is a vast and varying land where man has long made Nature his ally. Ten percent of the active population are engaged in agriculture. France has become the leading wheat producer in western Europe. Ranching is on a scale comparable with that of the United States in order to send 4 million tons of meat to the markets every year. Dairy farms annually yield 20 million hectolitres/440 million gallons of milk, and more than 300 kinds of cheese are manufactured. Vineyards stretch for hundreds of miles in the wine producing areas, producing 62 million hectolitres/1363 million gallons of wine in an average year.

France is a highly organized state, run by an efficient civil service, enjoying a truly universal educational system, practical welfare services and a steadily rising standard of living. Yet, devotion to the freedom of the individual has frequently meant political instability: it seems to need the strong hand of a Napoleon, Clemenceau or de Gaulle to organize every Frenchman's political awareness and create practical policies. A real patriot never goes unheard in France.

France is not a classless society. The urban populations of Paris and two or three other major cities, the inhabitants of the provincial towns, and the peasants in remote rural areas have entirely different modes of living. Yet no group is isolated from the other two. The most sophisticated and wealthy Parisian invariably keeps in close contact with his numerous relatives in provincial towns: he may even own a little piece of land somewhere deep in the countryside.

The old-fashioned family which has lived in a provincial town for generation after generation encourages and expects some of its members to excel in science, industry of commerce, and move to Paris. These migrants will become Parisians but they will also remain provincials.

And, Parisian or provincial, the bourgeois Frenchman will accept the fact that there's something of the peasant about him – and be proud of it. The peasant may be poor, simple and even reactionary, but he is still recognized as the true Frenchman.

Because of this mutual respect among the different classes the French excel in tolerance. A stranger is judged only on his merit as a human being. He may be unconventional in his personal life but if he is sincere, then he is entitled to his views and actions.

For the foreign visitor this deep respect for other people makes for happy times. Halting and mispronounced words do not result in a giggle. Demands for dishes similar to those at home will be met as best as can be, with the French sigh of mystification and regret well concealed. Peculiar requirements in shops will be satisfied if humanly possible. This is not because the French find the tourist trade profitable or because of innate courtesy towards a guest so much as an instinctive desire to live and let live.

Another major influence on the French way of life is the regard for the family. The grouping of persons with the same name, under the same roof, is to every Frenchman far more important than the personal happiness of any member of it. Even the young people of France, as 'with it' as any younger generation anywhere, accept that love is one thing, marriage another. The arranged marriage, fundamentally an economic partnership, still survives in France, and works out extremely well.

Perhaps uniquely among the nations of the West, France has discovered the secret of preparing for the twenty-first century without abandoning the past. The visible fabric is ultra-modern, but the foundation is tradition.

THE ARTS

Painting

The importance of France as a religious centre in the Middle Ages made the monasteries the main source of artistic effort. The loveliest illuminated psalters in existence were the work of monkish scribes in Paris in the 13th and 14th centuries. Schools to teach the craft were also set up in Burgundy and Avignon. Some of these men moved from their abbeys to design the stained glass and decorative metal work in the cathedrals being built at that time, and they also painted murals on the church walls.

In the early 16th century the growing wealth and power of the French monarchy and aristocracy enabled them to employ Italian artists to paint pictures for the châteaux. Thus French painters were influenced by the Italian style. Most notable was **Jean Fouquet** (*ca* 1415–85).

The 17th century marks the beginning of French influence on world art. **Nicolas Poussin** (1594–1665) originated the classical landscape, with gods and goddesses set in a natural environment. **Claude de Lorraine** (1600–82) made brilliant use of light in a manner perhaps since excelled only by Turner.

During the Golden Age of the French monarchy the great masters painted works which are now priceless. **Antoine Watteau** (1684–1721) depicted the luxury and laxness of the age with his pictures of amorous couples in gardens and woodlands. **Nicolas de Largillière** (1656–1746) flattered his patrons by painting their ladies as Olympian goddesses. In contrast, **Jean Chardin** (1699–1779) has left us a vivid glimpse of the ordinary people and of their homes in his bourgeois portraits and still-life studies. **Honoré Fragonard** (1732–1806) was at his best in female nudes and mythological figures. **Greuze** (1725–1805) captured the charm of youthful innocence.

But the greatest periods of French painting were still to come. The 19th century is never likely to be eclipsed in the rich spate of timeless works of art which can now be seen in the art galleries of the world. **David** (1748–1825) was an early master, the pioneer neo-classicist and founder of a new school of historical painting. This was a period of violent arguments among painters: classicism versus romanticism. **Pierre-Paul Prud'hon** (1758–1823) was the master in the former style and **Eugène Delacroix** (1798–1863) in the latter.

After the political upheavals of the Revolution and Napoleonic era painters could no longer rely on wealthy patrons. They painted for painting's sake. Portraits of the famous gave way to landscapes. **Corot** (1796–1875) was the first great master of the new school. He liked to include a female figure in his scene – unlike artists of the Barbizon school who were inspired by Dutch landscape artists. **Millet** (1814–75), **Theodore Rousseau** (1812–67) and **Daubigny** (1817–78) are the best of this group.

The public was both excited and disturbed by the new conception of artists, and never more than by **Manet** (1832–83), who adapted the themes of old masters with nudes and inferences which shocked Paris. Manet inspired young artists: the Impressionists. **Monet** (1840–1926) is the most celebrated, but **Renoir** (1841–1919), **Pissarro** (1830–1903), and **Dégas** (1834–1917) can rival him. The greatest collection of their works is in the Musée du Jeu de Paume in Paris.

Whatever misgivings reactionaries had about this group, still another revolutionary was at work. He was **Cézanne** (1836–1906), whose once hated pictures can now be seen as reproductions in millions of homes. Cézanne was the first of the moderns, showing the way to the primitives like **Gauguin** (1848–1903) and **Henri Rousseau** (1844–1910), and later **Braque** (1882–1963), **Matisse** (1869–1954), **Picasso** (1881–1973), and **Miro** (1893–1983).

The 19th-century French painters who dispensed with the restrictive conventions originating in the works of Italian and Flemish masters centuries before, had made Paris the unquestioned centre of painting. Many artists of the Paris School, like Picasso, were not French by birth, but only by adoption. By believing that art is international and gladly acting as host, France has made modern painters her protégés.

Architecture

If France has been the great patron of pictorial art she is the supreme genius of architecture. The inspiration for her early builders came from the many splendid monuments left by the Romans. The example of massive construction was followed by the Christian builders before the Romans left. Large churches had been built at Tours, Lyon and Clermont-Ferrand before the end of the 5th century. Later, both the Romanesque and Gothic styles were French developments.

In the 11th and 12th centuries Romanesque abbeys were being built all over the country, notably at Caen, Poitiers, Le Puy, Toulouse and Cluny. Well before the end of the century, the pointed arch of the Gothic style had appeared. The marriage of expert constructional knowledge and artistic genius gave birth to Notre Dame in Paris, and the cathedrals of Chartres, Reims, Amiens, Strasbourg and many more. Simultaneously, in contrast to the deceptive delicacy and fragility of the lofty churches, with tracery and sculpture, the great stone fortress-castles rose.

The Italian Renaissance was slow to influence French architects, but under the encouragement of King Francis I the novel designs were gradually adopted. The architects were responsible for many of the Loire châteaux, country residences rather than military outposts, and the Louvre in Paris. **Lemercier** (1580–1654), after studying in Italy, designed the Palais Royal and the Sorbonne in Paris early in the 17th century; **François Mansart** (1598–1666) built the Orléans wing at Blois. His great-nephew, **Jules Hardouin Mansart** (1646–1708) was patronized by Louis XIV and was responsible for the palace of Versailles.

In the 18th century a father and son were royal architects in succession. The father, **Jacques-Jules Gabriel** (1667–1742), was a great bridge builder and designed the façade of La Rochelle cathedral and the archbishop's palace at Blois; his son, **Ange-Jacques Gabriel** (1698–1782), made additions to Versailles, Fontainebleau and Choisy: he laid out the Place de la Concorde in Paris, and achieved immortality with his 'jewel', the Petit Trianon at Versailles.

Under Napoleon the conquests of France in Egypt and the desire to symbolize power resulted in buildings reminiscent of Athens, the Pharaohs and ancient Rome. The reaction was a brief Gothic revival, an unsatisfactory return to the past, soon followed by interest in functional architecture and the use of reinforced concrete. This revolution, since imitated all over the world, was the work of **Auguste Perret** (1874–1954). In his long life (he began practice in 1897) he was responsible for some remarkable churches (at Raincy and Montmagny) and the Champs-Elysées Theatre in Paris. A pupil of his was a Swiss, **Le Corbusier** (1887–1965), who settled in Paris in 1922 and became the founder of the Modern Movement in architecture. His memorial in France is the gigantic block of flats in Marseille, the Unité d'Habitation. The latest advance in France is the Centre Pompidou in Paris, designed by an Anglo-Italian team, **Rogers** and **Piano**.

Sculpture

French genius in sculpture can be seen outside and inside every Gothic cathedral. In the 14th century sculptors practised the art of realism in sepulchral effigies; to enhance the accuracy of the portrayal the recumbent figures were then carved upright. During the Renaissance, imitation of Greek and Roman styles in sculptures of mythological figures became usual. **Jean Goujon** (d. *ca* 1566) and **Jean Cousin** (*ca* 1522–94) were pre-eminent.

Louis XIV, with his limitless desire for grandeur, had art run like a government department. **Le Brun**, his personal painter, was director of various arts and crafts enterprises and rector of the Royal Academy of Sculpture. He was responsible for finding sculptors who could, in stone, create as accurate a likeness as a painter. **Coysevox** (1640–1720) was one of them. **Girardon** (1628–1715) was responsible for a large number of the sculptures in Versailles.

In the 18th century **Houdon** (1741–1828) was famous for portraiture. Among his well-known busts are those of Napoleon, Voltaire and Lafayette. He went to America to execute a monument of Washington.

François Rodin (1840–1917) was perhaps the most successful of any French sculptor. Casts of his work can be seen in every important museum the world over. *The Burghers of Calais, The Kiss, The Thinker, Eve* and *The Hand of God* are merely a few famous examples of his prodigious output, much of which can be seen in the Musée Rodin in Paris.

The Kiss: Rodin

CURRENCY

The unit of currency in France is the franc (F) which consists of 100 centimes. There are notes to the value of 5, 10, 50, 100 and 500 F, coins to the value of 1, 5, 10, 20, 50 centimes (also embossed $\frac{1}{2}$ F), and 1, 2, 5 and 10 F. You may import unlimited amounts of French currency and bank notes of other countries but check with your own bank what the restrictions are on exporting currency. You may not take more than 5000 F out of France. Travellers' checks are a valuable safeguard against theft, but it is advisable to have some French currency with you before entering the country.

Banking hours In large towns banks are open Mon. to Fri. from 0800–1200 and 1400–1630. Some may open 0930–1200 on Sat. and close on Mon. All banks are closed on Sun. and public holidays, most closing at 1200 on the previous day (see p. 27).

Main line railway stations in large towns, travel agencies and large hotels provide exchange facilities during the hours of the day when the banks are closed. They will display the sign *CHANGE.* Hotels may charge a rather higher service fee than banks. In Paris exchange offices are open at the Invalides air terminal and main line rail termini from 0730 to midnight; those at Orly, Charles de Gaulle and Le Bourget never close. The Accueil de France offices also provide exchange facilities (see p. 16). In large stores in the main towns payment by travellers' check can mean a discount for visitors from other than EEC countries. As long as they pay in travellers' checks they may take the goods with them or have them delivered direct to the aircraft or ship leaving France. This exemption from value added tax does not apply to visitors residing in the Common Market countries.

HOW TO GET THERE

Air Services

From London Heathrow: Bordeaux, Lyon, Marseille, Mulhouse-Basel, Nice, Paris (British Airways); Biarritz, Bordeaux, Lille, Lyon, Marseille, Montpellier, Nantes, Nice, Paris, Strasbourg, Toulouse (Air France).

From London Gatwick: Le Havre, Caen, Rennes, Morlaix, Quimper (BritAir); Paris (British Caledonian); Montpellier, Perpignan, Toulouse (Dan Air); Deauville (Lucas Air); Clermont-Ferrand (Touraine Air).

From London Stansted: Paris (Air UK).

From Birmingham: Paris (British Airways).

From Castle Donnington: Paris (British Midland Airways).

From Coventry: Paris (Air Commuter).

From Edinburgh: Paris (Air UK).

From Glasgow: Paris (British Airways).

From Jersey: Dinard, Le Touquet, Paris (Jersey European Airways); Cherbourg (Aurigny Air).

From Leeds/Bradford: Paris (Air UK).

From Manchester: Nice, Paris (British Airways); Paris (Air France).

From Plymouth: Brest, Morlaix (Brymon Airways).

From the USA: TWA, Pan Am, El Al, Northwest Orient, have direct flights to Paris from New York, Boston, Chicago, Los Angeles, Washington. In season there are direct flights New York–Nice.

Sea Ferries

Hovercraft services: Ramsgate–Calais (Hoverlloyd); Dover-Boulogne, Dover-Calais (Hoverspeed).

Passenger and car ferries:

Dover–Boulogne (Sealink, P & O).

Dover–Calais (Townsend Thoresen).

Dover–Dunkerque (Sealink).

Folkestone–Boulogne (Sealink).

Folkestone–Calais (Sealink).

Jersey–St-Malo (Emeraude Ferries).

Jersey and Guernsey–St-Malo (Condor hydrofoil – foot passengers only).

Newhaven–Dieppe (Sealink).

Plymouth–Roscoff (Brittany Ferries).

Portsmouth–Cherbourg and Le Havre (Townsend Thoresen).

Portsmouth–St-Malo (Brittany Ferries).

Ramsgate–Dunkerque (Sally Line).

Southampton–Le Havre (Townsend Thoresen; P & O).

Weymouth–Cherbourg (Sealink).

Corsica Marseille and Toulon–Ajaccio and Bastia. Nice to Bastia, Calvi, Île-Rousse. Early advance booking essential in summer. Enquiries SNCM, 179 Piccadilly, London W1Y 0BA.

Train and Boat

London (Victoria) via Dover and Boulogne hoverports – Amiens and Paris.

London (Charing X) via Dover and Boulogne hoverports – Amiens and Paris.

London (Victoria) via Folkestone and Calais – Amiens and Paris.

The Parisienne runs nightly as Inter-City European service from London (Waterloo) via Southampton and Le Havre to Paris. Connecting trains from Birmingham, Bristol, Cardiff, Coventry, Oxford, Reading and Wolverhampton to Southampton.

London (Victoria) via Folkestone and Calais – Valence, Avignon, Marseille, Toulon, St Raphaël, Cannes, Nice, Monte Carlo, Menton.

Coach Services

Euroways (7 York Way, London N1 9UD) run regular services from London to Aix-en-Provence, Amiens, Annecy, Antibes, Bayonne, Biarritz, Bordeaux, Cannes, Chambéry, Chamonix, Digne, Grasse, Grenoble, Lourdes, Lyon, Marseille, Montpellier, Nice, Pau, Perpignan, Tours.

Coach tours within France, lasting half day, whole day, or several days are organized by French Railways. Details from all stations in large towns.

The National Express Supabus runs daily from Bath, Birmingham, Bristol, and Southampton to Paris, with sea crossing Southampton–Le Havre. Connecting coaches from South Wales and West Country. Details from any National Express office.

IF YOU ARE MOTORING

Rules of the Road Traffic keeps to the right. Road markings are those used internationally. Pedestrians have right-of-way at crossings marked with studs. In built-up areas and at junctions the vehicle coming from the right has right-of-way, unless otherwise indicated. Vehicles on roundabouts have right-of-way.

Roads are classified as follows:

A–Autoroute (motorway), N–Route Nationale, D–Route Départementale. Some are being re-classified and re-numbered.

Warning triangle should be carried in case of breakdown or accident, and be placed 50m/55yd behind the obstruction.
Parking is forbidden where the vehicle

Use of the horn is forbidden in most towns, lights being flashed instead.
Yellow lamps are compulsory on French-owned cars; foreign motorists are advised to obtain yellow lamps or fit transparent yellow discs. British lamps must be adapted to dip to the right with lens converters or special stick-on strips. Dipped lights must be used at times of poor visibility; motorcyclists must use dipped lights even in daytime. All cars must have a left-hand external driving mirror. A complete set of spare bulbs for all lights must be carried.
Seat belts must be worn and children under ten may not travel in front seats unless there are no back seats. Motorcyclists and moped riders and their passengers must wear **crash helmets**.

would restrict the movement of traffic, at junctions and on bends where the view would be obstructed for passing traffic. In some towns a complete ban on parking is indicated by red paint on the kerb. In small towns and villages parking is allowed on one side of the street only; the side nearest to the buildings with even numbers for the first half of the month, and the side with the odd numbers for the second half. Some towns (including Paris) use the *zone bleu* system, usually allowing parking for one hour. The blue disc, available from police stations, service stations, newsagents and motoring organizations, is displayed on the windshield with figures indicating the time when parking began. Coin meters are numerous in large towns.

Speed limits, strictly enforced, are 130kph/81mph on autoroutes with tolls (110kph/68mph in wet weather); 110 kph/68mph on dual carriageways and by-pass autoroutes; 90kph/56mph on open roads (80kph/50mph in wet weather); 50kph/37mph in built-up areas. All limits are liable to change by indicator signs. Police may impose on-the-spot fines for infringement.

A driver holding a full driving licence for less than one year is restricted to 90kph/56mph and the vehicle must carry a sticker obtainable at any service station indicating this status. You may not drive on a provisional licence. The minimum age for driving either a car or a motorcycle over 125cc is 18.

Documents etc A valid driving licence and some form of identity (*eg* a passport) must always be carried, and produced on demand. Provisional licences are not recognized as valid. American motorists must obtain an International Driving permit from the AAA. The car registration book should also be carried for possible inspection at the port of entry. A national identity plate (GB, USA, *etc*) must be displayed on the rear of the vehicle. Vehicles equipped to carry more than nine persons must be fitted with a tachograph. The larger garages should be able to install one.

Insurance For nationals of Common Market countries Green Card insurance is not compulsory as it is for other visitors, but the policy obtained in Britain may provide only the minimum third party cover required by French law. It is therefore advisable to obtain a Green Card from your insurance company or broker before leaving for France, and check that your policy does not exclude overseas cover.

Accidents In the event of an accident, whether causing injury or only damage to a vehicle, obtain the names and addresses of witnesses and, if possible, take a photograph of the vehicle(s) involved. Local police will provide the name and address of a bailiff (*huissier*) who will prepare a written report, which is valuable in the event of a court case and for establishing responsibility involved in an insurance claim. The bailiff's fee varies according to the work involved, but charges are nationally controlled.

For immediate help dial 17 for police, 18 for ambulance.

Drink-drive Penalties Drivers with a level over 80mg/100ml must submit to a blood test. Penalties may include suspension of licence, heavy fine, or prison. Spot checks on all motorists can be enforced.

Fuel and Oil Fuel is supplied by the litre (4½ litres to the Imperial gallon). There are two grades: *ordinaire* (2-star) and *super* (4-star). All fuel is purchased by value as shown on the pump's meter. Oil is also supplied by the litre (just under 2 pints).

Car Rental International car rental firms, airlines and French Railways offer comprehensive schemes combining travel by ship, train or air with a self-drive car ready at the destination. French Railways have cars available at 200 stations, and bookings can be made at any station in a town of more than 20,000 inhabitants.

The names and addresses of a considerable number of car rental firms can be obtained from the National Automobile Chamber of Commerce, 6 rue Léonard-de-Vinci, Paris 16e (Tel: 502 19 10). The only document required is a driving licence, but you must be over 25. Third party, fire and theft insurance is always included in the hire charge.

Holiday Routes Yellow and green arrows indicate picturesque and uncongested routes. Service stations displaying the *bison futé* humorous sign will provide free maps of adjacent holiday routes.

Sea Ferries The ship services and some hovercraft ones listed on page 11 carry cars and trailers as well as passengers. Advance booking is essential in the tourist season. Addresses of carriers are on page 27.

Car Trains In France there are two versions of this service. Car-sleeper expresses run through the night with passengers in *couchettes* (four berths per compartment 1st class, six berths 2nd class) and the cars at the rear of the train on two-tier wagons. Most trains include sleeping cars with 1-, 2- and 3-berth compartments. Car-carrier trains run between the larger towns, passengers travelling by ordinary express, collecting their cars at the arrival station the next morning.

From Britain car-sleeper trains are: Calais – Narbonne, Nice; Boulogne – Brive, Biarritz, Narbonne, Bordeaux, Avignon, St Raphaël; Dieppe – Avignon, Marseille.

The principal internal car-train services run between Paris and Avignon, Biarritz, Bordeaux, Brive, Évian-les-Bains, Fréjus-St Raphaël, Gap, Grenoble, Lyon, Marseille, Narbonne, Nice, Nimes, St Gervais, Strasbourg, Toulon, Toulouse.

Motorail bookings made in advance in Britain are handled by French Railways' London office. Information can also be obtained and reservations made through British Rail and the motoring organizations.

INTERNAL TRAVEL

Railways The railway network of the Société National de Chemins de Fer (SNCF) has 37,000km/23,000mi of track serving more than 6000 stations. The main routes have some of the fastest trains in the world. There are two classes, 1st and 2nd, with 1st-class fares being some 50 percent more expensive. Mixed-class tickets can be obtained, allowing travel part of the way in 2nd class and part in 1st class.

For overnight trips (Paris to the Pyrenees: 6½hrs; Paris to the Riviera: 7½hrs), there are 1st and 2nd class *couchettes* or *wagon-lit* sleepers available. Most long-distance trains include a dining car. All main stops have good quick-service buffets and packaged meals are available from platform trolleys.

Trans-Europ Expresses link main towns at speeds averaging up to 145kph/90mph (1st class only plus a supplement). Advance reservation is always necessary.

On local lines service is maintained by diesel-powered rail cars. Even in remote areas there is rarely a long wait for this fast form of travel.

Any ticket bought in France must be date-stamped on the automatic machine at the platform entrance. Failure to do so may entail a surcharge after inspection on the train.

Many forms of price reduction exist for railway travel, including party, student, senior citizen and tourist tickets. Children travel free up to four years of age, and at half fare between four and ten (twelve on international ticket).

'France-Vacances' rover tickets, for unlimited travel over the entire French railway network, are available for 7 days or 15 days.

Railway tickets can be bought and seats reserved up to six months ahead in Britain. All accredited travel agents can arrange the purchase of tickets in advance.

Buses Bus services complete the links with every village and hamlet in France not served by railways, usually terminating at a railway station on a main line. Some of these services are run by French Railways and timetables are displayed outside the station, while details of routes and fares are available at the enquiry office inside.

Information on local bus services which are maintained by independent operators is obtainable at local tourist offices.

Buses in the sense of Britain's and America's long-distance services do not exist except on a few routes passing through a string of large towns which are not on a convenient railway route, *eg* Paris–Nice. In other words, there is no competition between road and rail as far as long-distance passenger services are concerned. But there are sightseeing tours, usually with a guide, in all the tourist centres. These range from a tour round the town to all-day excursions. Details from the local Syndicat d'Initiative.

Domestic Air Services Air-Inter operates scheduled air services to 30 different towns in France. On most routes the duration of the flight is one hour or less. Details of times and fares obtainable from any office of Air France, or from Air-Inter head office at 232 rue de Rivoli, 75001 Paris.

The following are the principal routes with frequent daily services:

Paris – Agen, Basel/Mulhouse, Biarritz, Bordeaux, Brest, Clermont-Ferrand, Corsica (Ajaccio, Bastia, Calvi), Grenoble, Limoges, Lorient, Lourdes/Tarbes, Lyon, Marseille, Metz, Montpellier, Mulhouse, Nancy, Nantes, Nice, Nîmes, Pau, Perpignan, Quimper, St-Étienne, Strasbourg, Toulon/Hyères, Toulouse.

Lyon – Basel/Mulhouse, Bordeaux, Clermont-Ferrand, Lille, Marseille, Metz, Nantes, Nice, Strasbourg, Toulouse.

Marseille – Basel/Mulhouse, Bordeaux, Corsica (Bastia, Calvi), Nice, Toulouse.

The following services operate in the holiday season:

Paris – La Baule, Deauville, St Raphaël/Fréjus, Vichy.

Nice – Vichy.

Lyon – St Raphaël/Fréjus.

A 'France-Pass' allowing unlimited travel on Air-Inter flights (valid for seven or fourteen days) is available for residents of USA, Canada, Japan, South Africa and Australia. Bookings through Air France and Air-Inter offices.

Regional airlines – Air Alsace, Air Littoral, Touraine Air, Languedoc Air – run short-haul services. Details from Syndicat d'Initiative, to be found in all large towns.

WHERE TO STAY

Hotels The 40,000 tourist hotels offer service and facilities which have passed the government's strict tests for classification. All such hotels bear a circular red, white and blue sign, usually alongside the main door, which bears the words COM-MISSARIAT GÉNÉRAL AU TOURISME and the date of the year when the check was made. The letters NN (*norme nouvelle*) indicate that the hotel has recently been regraded.

Stars indicate the category of the hotel as follows:

****	Top class
***	Very comfortable
**	Good average
*	Plain but comfortable

Each of these categories is sub-divided into A, B and C, so that there are 12 classifications. (There is a further special classification of ****L, which indicates a palatial de luxe establishment.)

One- to three-star hotels are bound by law to display the price of the room on the wall, and they must not charge more. But the displayed cost need not include the service charge or local taxes, though most of them add these details. These charges may increase the bill by 20 to 25 percent.

In France the charge is for the room, irrespective of the number of people involved. For this reason meals are charged separately, and usually the notice on the wall indicates the price of breakfast per person. Terms can, of course, be arranged in advance for weekly or longer periods, with reductions for children. Virtually all hotels serve breakfast, but not all provide other meals. Those with restaurants will usually quote prices for full pension (breakfast, lunch and dinner) or demi-pension (breakfast and lunch or dinner). It is impossible to quote prices with any accuracy. It can only be stressed that registered hotels are permitted to charge only what the government regards as a fair and reasonable figure for the services provided.

Châteaux Hotels and Relais de Campagne There are more than 150 of these establishments in France, all in beautiful houses or châteaux and surrounded by spacious grounds ensuring peace and tranquility. There are four categories, indicated on a sign in the form of a coloured shield:

Luxe	Exceptionally comfortable: luxurious service
****	Very comfortable: high standards
***	Good comfort: elegant simplicity
Rel.G.	Esteemed by gourmets for its food

The colour code is green for Relais de Campagne or Château, white for Relais en Montagne and pink for Relais Gourmand, enabling the tourist to choose the desired place in advance from the guide issued by Relais de Campagne, 14 rue de Constantine, F37000 Tours.

These establishments are all in the luxury class, particularly with regard to comfort and the cuisine. Necessarily the charges are high. Advance booking is essential in the busy season.

Logis de France and Auberges Rurales There are now 3700 modest 1- and 2-star hotels known as *logis*, found in every part of France except Paris. Most are situated in areas of natural beauty where there are few hotels. Government aid has been given to ensure that the rooms and facilities reach, and are maintained at, a good standard, and all provide generous meals if desired. The *auberges rurales* are in a similar organization which sets standards which are generally simpler than those of the logis. They are in villages, in contrast to the logis which are usually at a little distance from a rural community.

Both offer what is generally accepted as the best bargain for the tourist looking for economical accommodation. Their great popularity means that all rooms are invariably taken by late afternoon, and one should book in advance or call in person as soon after midday as possible. The Syndicat d'Initiative in any large town will have the addresses of all neighbouring logis and auberges in the scheme. A guidebook, brought up to date each February, can be ordered through bookshops or from the publishers Librairie Française Hachette, 4 Regent Place, London W1R 6BH.

Motels now exist in every region, some easily accessible from the autoroutes and main roads, but at a distance from the noise of traffic. Those serving the autoroutes are near Beaune, Mâcon, Nemours, Peronne, and Salon-de-Provence. Classification as for hotels, with letter 'M'.

Self-catering Accommodation The Gîtes Ruraux de France is an organization controlling and promoting facilities for guests to stay in the houses of farmers and villagers, furnished flats and houses in rural areas, and static trailers adjacent to farmhouses. No meals are provided, but cooking utensils and facilities, crockery, cutlery, bedding, *etc*, must reach an approved standard. Rentals are from a week to the entire season. Each department has its own bureau with a list of vacant accommodation. A London booking service is available to members of the Gîtes association. Annual fee includes a handbook listing more than 1800 sites. Details from Gîtes de France, 178 Piccadilly, London W1V 0AL. On request members can also receive lists of bed-and-breakfast addresses and hostels for overnight stops.

Tents and Trailers There are about 9000 registered camping sites in France, graded as follows:

****	First class low density sites
***	First class: emphasis on comfort
**	Good standard of amenities
*	Basic amenities

In addition there are the following specialized camps: luxury sites in the grounds of historic homes (list available from the French Government Tourist Office); first class sites usually offering static accommodation in trailers or bungalows (details from the Fédération Nationale de l'Hôtelerie de Plein Air, 10 ru de l'Isley, F75008 Paris); 43 sites run by the Touring Club de France (details from TCF, 6 Firmin-Gillot, 75015 Paris.)

The official camping and caravan guide, listing 8400 approved sites including farms, can be obtained from Hachette, 4 Regent Place, London W1R 6BH. Phone 01 734 5259 for current price.

Camping outside marked sites is not advisable without definite agreement from the farmer or landowner. Details of farms which regularly accept campers can be obtained from the Fédération Nationale des Syndicats d'Exploitantes Agricoles, 8 rue Marceau, F75008 Paris. Applicants should be members of a recognized camping organization.

Camping in ostensibly public countryside or the State forests is possible with permission from the local office of the government department concerned (enquire at the nearest Syndicat d'Initiative). It must be stressed that penalties for camping without permission, particularly in wooded areas, can be severe.

The gross weight of a caravan must not exceed the kerb weight of towing vehicle. Maximum width 2.5 metres, length 11 metres. Speed limits as for other traffic, but a minimum gap of 50 metres between towing vehicle and vehicle ahead must be observed. Overnight parking in any lay-by is forbidden. Vehicles towing caravans are prohibited in Paris.

Information All details of every kind of accommodation are readily obtainable from the information bureaux known as the Syndicats d'Initiative. In every town, large and small, and in many villages, there is one of these offices.

Booking The French rarely book far in advance at a hotel. Summer reservations made almost as soon as the New Year begins, bewilder the average French hotelier. The practice can be a source of mutual annoyance. Many small hotels close in the winter, and correspondence may be unread. Enclose an international reply coupon when booking.

The Accueil de France offices in some of the tourist centres can provide details of hotels, gîtes, camping sites, *etc*, as well as reservations for one to five days in advance, both in the town and the surrounding area. Towns, addresses, and areas: *Paris*: 127, Champs-Élysées. Paris area and whole of France. *Aix-les-Bains*: Place Maurice Mollard. Savoy and Dauphiny Alps. *Angers*: Place President Kennedy. Mayenne and southern Normandy. *Avignon*: 41 Cours Jean Jaurès. Central Provence. *La Baule*: 8 Place de la Victoire. Brittany coast. *Besançon*: Place 1ère Armée Française. Franche-Comté and Jura. *Blois*: Pavillon Anne de Bretagne, Avenue Jean Laigret. Loire valley. *Bordeaux*: Place Quinconces. Aquitaine and Dordogne. *Caen*: Place-St Pierre. Normandy. *Cannes*: Gare SNCF. Riviera. *Dijon*: Place Darcy. Burgundy. *Évian-les-Bains*: Place d'Allinges. Haute Savoie. *Grenoble*: rue de la République. French Alps. *Limoges*: Boulevard Fleurus. Limousin. *Lyon*: Place Bellecour. Rhône valley. *Marseille*: 4 la Canebière. Mediterranean coast. *Metz*: Porte Serpenoise. NE France. *Nancy*: 14 Place Stanislas. Lorraine. *Nantes*: Place du Change. Vendée. *Nice*: 32 au d'Hôtel-des-Postes. Riviera. *Le Puy*: Place du Breuil. Upper Loire. *Reims*: 3 Boulevard de la Paix. Champagne. *La Rochelle*: 11 bis rue des Augustins. Charente coast. *Rouen*: 25 Place de la Cathédrale. Central Normandy. *Strasbourg*: Palais des Congrès, Avenue Schutzenberger. Alsace. *Toulon*: 8 Avenue Colbert. Mediterranean coast. *Toulouse*: Donjon du Capitole. Mid-Pyrénées. *Tours*: Place du Maréchal LeClerc. Loire valley and châteaux. *Vichy*: 19 rue du Parc. Massif Central.

ENJOY YOURSELF

(An international reply coupon should be enclosed with any enquiry to addresses given in this section.)

Water Sports Canoeing is a popular recreation on stretches of the Loire Rhône, Isère and the streams and rivers in the mountainous regions of the Alps and Pyrenees. In all riverside communities of any size local canoe-kayak clubs give advice and facilities to visitors with proven experience. In addition courses of instruction are arranged in many areas both for beginners and more advanced participants by the Youth Section of the Touring Club de France. Details from its offices at 65 Avenue de la Grande Armée

75016 Paris. The national association which can give details of accommodation, *etc*, in specific areas is the Fédération Française de Canoe/Kayak, 87 Quai de la Marne, 94340 Joinville (Haute Marne).

River boats with living accommodation are available for hire on the Seine and Oise (Paris region), the canals of Brittany, Burgundy and the Rhône and Garonne zones. A licence to handle a powered vessel is necessary.

River and canal cruises are regularly run on the Loire, Dordogne, Rhône and Tarn. These, while usually lasting a full day, are not normally maintained by vessels with living accommodation. Those with bunks and meal facilities run on the Nivernais canal, the Canal du Midi and the Rhine (from Strasbourg).

Information regarding advance bookings, addresses of concessionaries, *etc* is available from the French Government Tourist Office.

Those taking their boats to France by sea may berth only at a port with a Customs office. A ship's passport must be obtained from the club or association of which the owner is a member. Pleasure craft for the owner's sole use may sail in French coastal waters or on inland waterways for a total of six months in any twelve months if they are covered by a certificate of registration and/or the Small Ships Register (SSR) document for boats under 24m/79ft in length. British craft do not need to have a *Permis de Circulation*.

Navigable waterways extend for 7500km/6570mi. Most attractive areas are on the Loire, Mayenne and Sarthe in western France; the Gironde, Garonne, and Lateral and Midi canals in the south west; Bourgogne and Nivernais canals, Saône and Rhône in the east and south east. Full information from Yachting Dept., French Government Tourist Office.

Many sailing schools exist around the coast, both for those bringing their own boats or using the schools' boats. Details from Fédération Française de Yachting à Voile, 70 rue St Lazare, 75009 Paris.

France was the first European country to develop waterskiing, thanks largely to the prevalence of inland lakes and the long Mediterranean coast. There are waterskiing clubs to be found in all Mediterranean resorts, including those in Corsica, and around the larger lakes. Details of clubs welcoming visitors and the best sites obtainable from Fédération Française de Ski Nautique, 9 Boulevard Pereire, 75017 Paris.

The best coast on which surfing is possible is around the Gulf of Gascogne between Bayonne and Hendaye on the Spanish border. The sport is controlled by the Fédération Française de Surf, Avenue Edouard VII, 64200 Biarritz.

Skin diving and snorkel diving are very popular sports around the coasts of Brittany, the Côte d'Azur, Provence and Corsica. Clubs exist in all the major resorts in these areas. Information: local Syndicats d'Initiative. Visitors are advised to contact these clubs, not only because of the need for advice about suitable areas and dangerous currents, *etc*, but also to ascertain local regulations. In the Mediterranean there are now restrictions on some kinds of underwater fishing or tampering with the submarine environment, and a fishing permit is usually needed.

Hunting, Shooting and Fishing The open season is from September to January or March depending on the quarry and the region. Non-residents in France must hold a licence or a permit for hunting and shooting. The licence is obtainable from the local police station in the district where the visitor intends to hunt and is valid for 48 hours. A hunting and/or shooting permit from the applicant's own country must be shown, together with two photographs, proof of identity and an insurance policy issued in France for hunting and shooting. The permit requires the same documents plus a certificate from a responsible person as to the applicant's good conduct. This permit is valid for the season. Information from Office National de la Chasse, 85 bis Avenue de Wagram, 75017 Paris, or from Office National de Forêts, 4 Avenue de St Mande, 75012 Paris.

The most popular outdoor recreation of the typical Frenchman is fishing, encouraged by the large number of rivers and lakes as well as the vast coastline. No permit is needed for fishing from the land or a boat along the maritime coast. In rivers, lakes and ponds local fishing federations are in control of individual societies in the area, the latter issuing permits which cost from 10 to 50F. The local Syndicat d'Initiative can provide the addresses of the societies in its area, or information can be obtained from the Conseil Superieur de la Pêche, 10 rue Peclet, 75010 Paris.

Mountaineering, Rock Climbing and Walking Mountain guides are available at Gavarnie, Luchon and St-Lary for the Mid-Pyrénées; Bastia for Corsica; Briançon, La Chapelle, La Grave, Embrun and Pelvoux for the High Alps; Chamonix and St-Gervais for the Savoie-Dauphiné.

Rock climbing, with local clubs giving advice and tuition, is an attraction in

Aquitaine (club at Périgueux); Auvergne (Clermont-Ferrand); Burgundy (Châlon-sur-Saône, Dijon, Mâcon); Corsica (Bastia); Fontainebleau Forest (Paris); Languedoc-Roussillon (Perpignan); Mid-Pyrénées (Montauban, Toulouse); Poitou-Charentes (Angoulême, Poitiers); Provence (Marseille); Côte d'Azur (Cannes, Nice). Personal application at the Syndicat d'Initiative in the towns listed above will provide addresses of clubs and schools. General information on both mountaineering and rock climbing may be obtained from Club Alpin Française, 7 rue la Boëtie, 75008 Paris.

More than 10,000km/6200mi of foot-paths and lanes have been marked for long-distance **walking holidays** covering the entire country. All avoid towns, main roads and industrial areas, taking the visitor into a France no motorist will see.

The footpaths are marked with small red and white directional signs, with blue symbols for hotel, shelter, camping site, water source, viewpoint, and so on. Itineraries run from one side of France to the other, north to south or east to west. There are also circular itineraries requiring one to three weeks' walking, covering a district, a mountain area or a coastal zone.

A list of Topo Guides is obtainable from the Comité National des Sentiers, 92 rue de Clignacourt, 75883 Paris, Cedex 18.

Caving Observance of local regulations and club rules is essential, but it will be found that properly equipped and experienced cavers are given a real welcome.

The best centres for making contact with local clubs (apply at local Syndicat d'Initiative for addresses) are Périgueux for the Dordogne; Clermont-Ferrand for Auvergne; Ajaccio for Corsica; Montpellier, Nîmes and Perpignan for South-West France; Toulouse and Foix for the Mid-Pyrénées; Marseille, Aix-en-Provence and Arles for Provence; Cannes and Nice for the Côte d'Azur; Grenoble for Savoie-Dauphiné.

Detailed information can be obtained from the Fédération Française de Spéléologie, 130 rue St Maur, 75011 Paris.

Skiing France has the largest number of ski resorts in Europe. Principal areas are Northern Alps (38 centres), Southern Alps (13), Pyrenees (8), Massif Central (3), Jura (2), and Vosges (2). Details of resorts from Comité des Stations Françaises de Sports d'Hiver, 36 rue de Bassano, 75008 Paris, or Fédération Française de Ski, 34 rue Eugène Flachat, 75017 Paris.

Cycling There are only minor formalities in taking a non-motorized cycle to France thanks to the national enthusiasm for cycling, and on many routes special cycle tracks have been laid down. Cycles can be rented at 140 railway stations in resort areas, whether the tourist arrives by train or not, and cycle rental shops exist in virtually every town and many villages.

Organized cycle tours, usually with accommodation in youth hostels or modest auberges, are available in every region through the local cycling club. Details from the Fédération Française de Cyclotourisme, 8 rue Jean Marie Jégo, 75013 Paris, and Le Bicyclub de France, 7 rue Ambroise Thomas, 75009 Paris.

Golf The best and most numerous 18-hole golf courses are adjacent to the popular coastal resorts and in the Ile-de-France. Many on the coast are part of the attractions offered by the hotels which own them; others are owned by the local authority. Details of temporary membership obtainable from the Fédération Française de Golf, 11 rue de Bassano, 75016 Paris.

Riding The enthusiast has a variety of holidays available—pony trekking, accompanied rides from special stables, riding tuition for adults and children. There are more than 500 centres covering every region, with guides, instructors and accommodation, and a variety of holidays which usually include arrangements for entertainment and tours as a contrast to the daily period of riding. Categories are free rides (camping with tent), country rides (accommodation at a farm), comfort rides (accommodation at a hotel).

There are 22 regional associations controlling tourists' horse riding holidays. A brochure giving their addresses, together with the riding centres and stables in each region, can be obtained from the Association Nationale pour le Tourisme Equestre et l'Equitation de Loisirs, 12 rue du Parc Royal, 75003 Paris.

Gliding and hang-gliding clubs cater for visitors in many coastal and hilly areas. The international centre is at Issoire (Puy-de-Dôme) and the competition for the European Cup takes place during the last two weeks of July at Angers (Maine-et-Loire). Full details of clubs' addresses, with arrangements for visitors, are available from the Fédération Française de Vol à Voile, 29 rue de Sèvres, 75006 Paris.

Working Holidays Temporary jobs, on farms, in shops, hotels, restaurants and cafés are sometimes available by enquiring locally, but competition from French applicants is acute.

There is now freedom of movement for workers within the Common Market countries. Check on opportunities, permits, *etc*, from the French Embassy, 58 Knightsbridge, London SW1.

Working Holidays, from good bookshops, is a factual annual published by the Central Bureau for Educational Visits and Exchanges, Seymour Mews, London W1, where personal callers can obtain advice.

American citizens are not allowed to enter France to take up employment without proof of a job and a long-stay visa. For further information contact The French Embassy, 2535 Belmont Road, NW Washington D.C. 2008.

Young People's Visits Although there are now more than 300 youth hostels (open May-September) in France the size of the country means that many are a considerable distance apart. But the majority are situated in areas which are of scenic beauty and attractive to walkers and cyclists, and with forward planning a good holiday using nothing but youth hostels can easily be arranged.

It must be stressed that in order to make use of youth hostels and the many other facilities available in France to young people (aged 15 to 30) an International Youth Hostels membership card must be held. This is obtainable after filling in the application form from the Youth Hostels Association, 14 Southampton Street, London WC2E 7HY, the Fédération Unie des Auberges de Jeunesse, 6 rue Mesnil, 75016 Paris, or American Youth Hostels Inc., 'I' Street NW, Suite 800, Washington D.C. 20005.

French government policy is to facilitate in every possible way cultural and recreational visits by groups of adolescents and young adults. Such groups can obtain accommodation through the following organizations:

Accueil des Jeunes en France, 12 rue des Barres, 75004 Paris, has more than 4000 beds in the provinces both for individual visitors and groups, as well as accommodation in Paris (see below).

Fédération des Maisons des Jeunes et de la Culture, 25 rue la Condamine, 75007 Paris, is mainly for organized groups, including those with young people under 15.

Organisation Centrale des Camps et Activities de la Jeunesse, 20 Boulevard Poissonnière, 75009 Paris is for organized groups wanting to camp as well as use hostels, schools, *etc*.

A stay in Paris need not be expensive. There are two youth hostels in the city and nine in the surrounding district. Youth centres in the city number 16 and offer 3500 beds in simple, clean accommodation, controlled by Accueil des Jeunes in France. More than 100 camping sites close

to the centre of Paris welcome young people. Details are available in a brochure issued by the Touring Club de France, 65 Avenue de la Grande Armée, 75782 Paris. The Union des Centres de Rencontres Internationales de France (UCRIF), 20 rue J. J. Rousseau, 75001 Paris, issues a full list of all youth centres throughout France.

Wine Tasting and Grape Harvesting Visitors to France in the period June-September will find a ready welcome in vineyards in the major wine-producing areas, often with a multilingual guide and wine tasting for a nominal fee. Roads leading to the great estates are marked *Route du Vin* or *Route des Grands Crus*. The best regions for this sort of tour are Alsace, Bordeaux, Burgundy, Champagne, the Jura and the Loire valley.

The grape-picking season starts in mid-September and lasts about a month. The work is quite hard but little skill is required and a modest daily wage is paid. Food and lodging are free. Information can be obtained from the Maison des Jeunes, BP26, 25 rue des Vosges, 11200 Lezignan Corbières (for South-West France) or Centre des Jeunes Agriculteurs de la Gird Gironde, 13 rue Foy, 33 Bordeaux.

Railways Enthusiasts of the 'steam horse' and its successors can combine their interest with a comprehensive tour of France. Apart from inspecting or travelling on some of the 1130 *rapide* and *express* trains scheduled every day, they will find a surprisingly large number of historic locomotives and rolling stock run on preserved railways.

Typical are the 6km/3¾mi line starting from Pithiviers (Loiret) hauled by an 1870 engine, and the carriages built in 1900 on the steam train of Cappy (Somme). Most of these trains operate only in the summer and some only at weekends. Information from Fédération des Amis des Chemins de Fer Secondaires, 27 rue de Colombes, 92600 Asnières.

War Graves and Memorials In the north of France, along the Normandy coast and inland, there are many reminders of the battles of the Second World War; emplacements, observation forts, now part of the landscape, and many monuments. There is a *Guide Bleu* to the area and events of the Normandy landings but most of the permanent markers of the action speak for themselves.

For further information contact The Commonwealth War Graves Commission, 2 Marlow Road, Maidenhead, Berks, (Tel: 0628 34221); The American Battle Monuments Commission, Room 2067, Temple A, Second District, SW

Washington D.C. 20315. Inquirers seeking a particular grave should provide the full name and any service details known of the deceased.

Conservation and Natural History Sixteen national and regional nature conservation parks are maintained in areas of exceptional beauty. They offer inexhaustible interest to the nature lover, ornithologist, photographer, botanist and walker. Many of the parks are uninhabited and rich in fauna and flora. All are subject to strict controls. Permitted activities within the parks should be checked at the entrance building.

Prehistory Few countries in Europe are so rich in traces of early man as France. For the visitor with limited time at his disposal, the richest area is in Périgord-Quercy between Montignac and Cahors, where sites cover 200,000 years of man's early history. At some sites there are organized tours daily during the summer with multilingual guides. Details from the local Syndicat d'Initiative.

Naturism France was the first country to advance the idea of the beneficial effects of sunshine and air on the human body, and pioneered tolerance as regards near-nudity and nudity in specified resorts. Principal ones are Cap d'Agde ('nude city'), Port-Leucate and Montalivet. The 'monokini' (topless sunsuit or swimsuit) is accepted on most beaches along the Mediterranean coast. In Corsica nudity is restricted to beaches in the vicinity of Alistro and Porto Vecchio. (Information from Club Naturiste Corse, Pastrucciale, par San Nicolas 20, Corsica.)

There are also scores of naturist clubs, many of which welcome visitors who are accredited members of naturist clubs in other countries. Addresses can be obtained from the Fédération Française de Naturisme, 4 Avenue du Coq, 75009 Paris.

Health Spas France has 100 major health spas and more than 1200 mineral springs, for centuries used for medical treatment of specific diseases and general recuperation and physical toning. Details of all spas are obtainable from the Fédération Thermale et Climatique Française, 8 Avenue de l'Opéra, Paris.

EATING AND DRINKING

Even though France has accepted the existence of 'convenience foods', the traditional pride in good food ensures that individuality remains the uncontested attraction of a French meal. The independent shops and the street markets flourishing in every town, large or small, are still the mainstay of food supply both to private households and restaurants.

Eating out in France is quite expensive, mainly because quality and quantity are the considerations rather than price. But value for money is good, whether one eats in a luxury establishment, a corner café, a bistro, a self-service cafeteria or, in the country, a *relais routiers* (truck drivers' restaurant).

Generally speaking, at midday and in the evening, the French expect several courses, each purporting 'to eat the other' so that contrast in flavour and substance makes it possible to eat more than one would imagine. However, most restaurants are ready to serve one course on the welcome policy that the customer is always right.

If you want a complete meal of good quality and at a competitive price you can patronize a Tourist Restaurant, marked by a square panel with a white R on a blue circle. White stars indicate the category:

Luxe et ****	Luxury establishment
***	First class
**	Medium menu
*	Family restaurant

All these restaurants offer a daily tourist menu of traditional dishes (except the luxury category where a special menu is not obligatory). The tourist menu must be displayed outside the premises, with the price, whether service and drink are included or are extra, and usually one alternative to the main course. The meal, at midday or in the evening, consists of hors d'oeuvre or soup, a main course and cheese or fruit. Apart from the guarantee of quality of food and cooking, the tourist restaurant must conform to standards as regards service, toilet facilities and cloakrooms.

Compared with the huge number of eating places in the country, tourist restaurants are not numerous in towns where the flow of tourists would not justify proprietors joining the organization. This has no significance, and competition ensures that one can always get a meal at an acceptable price with dishes of one's choice.

Water from a tap directly joined to the mains is always pure and drinkable. Taps in public places supplying non-drinkable water are, by law, marked *eau non potable*. Water from the cold tap in a hotel bedroom may not be completely safe if it comes from the mains via a storage tank at the top of the building.

Cafés and restaurants will readily supply a glass of water if asked, but such a demand is unusual. It is the custom to ask for bottled water, which is very cheap (the main cost when buying a bottle to take away is the – returnable – charge on the bottle itself). All these bottled waters come from France's spas and contain no added ingredient. They may be slightly effervescent, slightly bitter or sweet.

Tea is now widely drunk and can be ordered at any time of the day in any café. Unless one specifies *au lait* it will be served with a slice of lemon. Tea bags are always used, and because of the French habit of drinking tea without milk the brew will be weak, at least by British standards. Add a tea bag of your own to the pot.

Coffee is the universal hot drink. The strongest and cheapest is a small cup from an expresso machine, the best and most expensive from a filter placed on a large cup. *Café nature* is black coffee; *café au lait* or *café crème* is with milk in a separate jug or whipped cream; *café complet* is coffee with hot milk, a roll and butter.

Cold soft drinks include national brands of flat or fizzy diluted fruit syrups and, of course, the ubiquitous colas. The most refreshing are natural orange and lemon fresh fruit juices – *orange/citron pressé* – served after the juice has been extracted in a blender or at the table with a squeezer so that the customer can prepare his own drink. Ice, sugar and water are brought to complete the preparation.

Aperitifs are drunk by the French before luncheon or dinner, in the belief that they sharpen the appetite and aid the digestion. There can be no doubt about the names of the popular aperitifs – their advertisements can be seen on every roadside billboard and in every café. They are far cheaper than scotch or gin. If either of these are ordered the glass will hold about double the usual British 'single'. If a small scotch is wanted, it should be ordered as a *bébé*.

Famous local wines have been mentioned where appropriate in the regional sections. While there is no need to order wine with a meal – and it will be immediately noticeable that many French people do not do so, especially at midday – it really should be included when enjoying a truly French meal. The great thing is to select the wine for which the district is known and not to take the easiest way by ordering a bottle with a familiar name. There is virtually no limit to the price which can be paid, but for most people a request for a bottle of the *vin du pays* (local wine) specifying red, white or rosé, or the economical carafe (containing enough for

three or four glasses) will not harm the pocket and will please the palate.

Those who yearn for a glass of beer as they know it, can have it – at a price. In the tourist areas most large cafés stock imported beers; they are usually of a higher alcoholic content. French beer is light and thirst-quenching. It is about half the price of the imported beer or lager. There are two kinds- *blonde* (light) and *brune* (dark).

Cider, very popular throughout northern France, is usually sold from barrels. It is the cheapest alcoholic drink in France when bought 'on the spot' in Brittany or Normandy. It is less gassy than the bottled ciders of Britain.

After-dinner liqueurs are numerous, apart from the famous cognac and armagnac. Some to try – and perhaps buy a bottle to take home – include Ratafia (acacia flowers), Cassis (blackcurrants), Chartreuse (herbs), Menthe (peppermint), Genièvre (juniper berries), Cerises (cherries), Noyaux (peach and apricot stones), Framboises (raspberries), Anis (aniseed).

SELF-CATERING SHOPPING

Street markets are held on weekday mornings two or three times a week in every city, town and village, selling vegetables, fruit, poultry, eggs and dairy products, always fresh and for the most part locally produced by the stallholder. Prices are usually lower than in shops.

Boulangerie (baker) Hot fresh bread on sale from 0700. Prices are controlled, and current prices for the bewildering array of breads are always displayed. Usually open on Sunday morning. Closed Monday.

Crémerie (dairy) Milk, butter and cheese. All milk is pasteurized and there are two grades, plus skimmed milk. Open Sunday morning, closed all day Monday.

Charcuterie (delicatessen) Cooked and ready-to-cook meats, eggs, sausages, pâtés and mixed dishes in enormous variety. No objection to an order for small amounts, and no need to specify weight, but to ask for so many slices. Many are open seven days a week (closed Sunday afternoon).

Marchand de légumes (greengrocer) There are not many of these establishments because of the prevalence of street markets. Most of them sell bottled water and soft drinks as well as imported fruit and the more exotic vegetables. Open Sunday morning. Closed all or half-day Monday except in tourist resorts.

Pâtisserie (cake shop) Cakes, tarts and confectionery. Most of the products are made on the premises and are of high quality but expensive. Open weekdays.

Pharmacie (chemist) Baby foods, patent medicines, first aid items and toilet goods. Virtually all pharmacies are independent businesses and the owner will be helpful in recommending, and probably compounding, something for the relief of minor troubles. Open weekdays.

Supermarket and Hypermarket Supermarkets exist in every town and have very good food sections, selling not only branded and pre-packed products but also the invariably cheaper local fresh products. Hypermarkets selling everything, including food, tend to be in the countryside outside large towns and have extensive parking space. Open weekdays 0800–2100; some open Sunday mornings.

WHAT YOU NEED TO KNOW

Passports A standard British 30 page passport costs £15 (husband and wife £22.50), 94 page passport £30 (husband and wife £45), after application on form obtainable at any main Post Office. A visitor's passport, valid for one year, costs £7.50 (husband and wife £11.25) after application on form from any main Post Office. For a standard passport two photos, proof of identity, and endorsement by a person of standing are required. Completed applications and fee must be sent to a Passport Office in London, Belfast, Glasgow, Liverpool, Newport (Gwent) or Peterborough, according to applicant's area as shown on the form. Application should be made at least four weeks in advance of journey. A visitor's passport is issued by personal application, with completed form, proof of identity, and two photographs, at any main Post Office in England, Wales, and Scotland, and at the Passport Office, 47 High Street, Belfast for Northern Ireland residents.

Persons who are citizens of the UK by naturalization or registration should check in advance that their passports are acceptable to the French authorities.

American citizens should apply in person to the US Passport Agency in New York, Boston, Chicago, Miami, New Orleans, San Francisco, Washington, or to the local courthouse. Two photographs of approved size, birth certificate, and proof of US citizenship are required. Cost $12. No re-entry permit is required if absence from the US is under 12 months.

Health certificates are not required for entry into France. Vaccination certificates are not required for re-entry into the UK or USA unless infection has been reported in the countries concerned.

Health Britain, as a member of the EEC, has an agreement with France that medical advice and treatment will be provided on the same basis as for French subjects. British visitors to France must have a certificate indicating that they are entitled to medical benefits under the British National Health Service. The certificate, form E111, is issued by the local offices of the Department of Health and Social Security, which will first require the application form CM1 to be completed. An explanatory leaflet, SA36, is issued with the certificate E111. It is advisable to have a photocopy made of your certificate as the original may be temporarily kept by the doctor, *etc.*

If medical aid is required while in France form E111 should be presented to the nearest Social Security Office (Caisse Primaire d'Assurance-Maladie), the address of which can be obtained from the police station, post office or *mairie* (town hall), or, in case of urgent need for treatment, from the doctor (or dentist). In Paris: Caisse Primaire Centrale d'Assurance-Maladie de la Région Parisienne, Centre 461, 84 rue Charles Michels, 93525 St-Denis, (Tel: 8206105). Ask for *Service des Relations Internationales*.

It is important to realize that the doctor, and the chemist who makes up any prescription, has to be paid by the patient. The doctor enters the amount of his fee and indicates that he has been paid, giving a copy of the prescription. The chemist will enter the cost of any medicines purchased on that prescription.

On presentation of form E111, the receipted sickness document and the copy of the prescription, the local Social Security Office will refund part of the cost – but only about 75 percent of it in normal circumstances. It should be stressed that medical expenses incurred overseas cannot be reimbursed by the British National Health Service on the patient's return to the UK.

When hospital treatment is necessary it is essential that the local Social Security Office and hospital be immediately informed that the patient is an insured person and holds form E111. Expenses are paid direct to the hospital by French Social Security, but again the patient is expected to pay a proportion of the bill, usually about 20 percent.

It will be obvious, in view of the necessity of meeting part of the cost of treatment or illness or injury, that the modest premium needed for insuring against these risks is a wise investment. It might also be pointed out that routine policies held to cover medical expenses in Britain do not always apply when abroad.

American visitors should check that their health insurance policy covers them when abroad. The additional cover necessary can be obtained through an insurance broker or travel agent.

Rabies Rabid wild animals, principally foxes, are at large in some parts of France. Caution is essential when approaching any wild animals, or dogs roaming free from control. There is at present no effective preventive vaccine against rabies. A bite or scratch incurred through contact with a wild or stray animal should be washed immediately with soap and water. Apply alcohol swab if possible and go to the nearest doctor or hospital.

The UK totally prohibits the importation of animals (including domestic pets) except under licence. One of the conditions of the licence is that the animals are retained in approved quarantine premises for up to six months. No exemptions are made for animals that have been vaccinated against rabies. Penalties for smuggling involve imprisonment, unlimited fines and the destruction of the animal.

Any animal being imported into the US must have a valid certificate of vaccination against rabies.

For details apply to the Ministry of Agriculture (Animal Health Division), Hook Rise South, Tolworth, Surbiton, Surrey KT6 7NF.

CB Radios Temporary importation is allowed for visitors holding a British Telecom licence to operate on 26.960–27.280 Mhz, with power not over 2 watts and maximum number of channels 220.

Customs On returning home you must declare everything.

Britain operates a two-tier scale of duty-free allowances: one for goods purchased in non-EEC countries or from a duty-free shop (even in an EEC country), and one for purchases from one of the EEC countries – France, Belgium, West Germany, Luxembourg, Italy, the Netherlands, Denmark, Ireland and Greece – where local taxes have already been paid (see below).

Duty-free allowances for UK residents *subject to change*

		Goods bought in a duty-free shop	Goods bought in France
Tobacco	Cigarettes or	200	300
	Cigars *small* or	100	150
	Cigars *large* or	50	75
	Pipe tobacco	250 g	400 g
Alcohol	Spirits *over 38.8° proof* or	1 litre	1½
	Fortified or sparkling wine or	2 litres	3 litres
	Table wine	2 litres	4 litres
Perfume		50 g	75 g
Toilet water		¼ litre	375 cl
Other goods*		£28	£163

* To include not more than 50 litres of beer

US customs permit duty-free $400 retail value of purchases per person, 1 litre of liquor per person over 21, 200 cigarettes and 100 cigars per person.

The allowances for tobacco and alcohol apply only to travellers over 17.

US customs permit duty-free $400 retail value of purchases per person, 1 litre of liquor per person over 21, 100 cigars and 200 cigarettes per person.

Exemption from VAT is available for visitors from countries outside the EEC on purchases of 125F or over. Prohibition of importation to the UK applies to counterfeit coins of any country, drugs such as opium, cannabis, LSD and amphetamines; live animals; firearms and ammunition, flick knives; plants, bulbs and certain vegetables and fruits; radio transmitters (including walkie-talkies); some meat and poultry raw or not fully cooked.

Postage Post offices are recognizable by the sign of a blue dart on a white disc and the letters PTT. They are open from 0800 to 1900 Mon.–Fri., 0800 to 1200 Sat. In cities the main post office will be open on Sundays and public holidays.

There is no need to visit the post office for stamps. They can be bought at the hotel, at tobacconists, and in most shops selling postcards. Letters for UK need a 2F.10 stamp for the first 20g (about ⅓oz); postcards, 1F.60. European letter mail goes by air; for USA and Canada air mail is 3F.25 for 5g. Rates liable to change.

Post boxes are coloured yellow. They are fixed to walls, and can easily be missed. A plaque on the front indicates the time of the next collection.

Telephones There are few public booths except in post offices and cafés. The system is steadily being made automatic, but in many rural areas it is usual for an operator to get the desired number. If the booth is painted blue it is for local calls; yellow booths serve the inter-town and grey the international lines. Most of these phones take coins of 20 centimes, 50 centimes, 1F and 5F, but there are still the older types for which a *jeton* (disc) must be used. Jetons can be bought from the café proprietor or post office. For UK numbers first dial 1944, wait for second dialling tone, and then dial the UK STD code, always omitting the first 0, followed by exchange and subscriber's number.

Electricity The standard supply is 220 volts 50 cycles AC. A few remote areas are on 110 volts AC, so a check should be made before plugging in electric shavers, hair dryers, travelling irons, *etc*. Usually a razor plug is fixed alongside the wash basin in hotel bedrooms, and normally the voltage will be clearly marked. Razors may need an adaptor for continental plugs (sold by all good electrical stores in Britain and the US).

Closing Days and Times Museums an art galleries are usually open from 1000 1700 in Paris, 1000 to 1200 and 1400 1600 elsewhere. Many close one weekda each week – usually Tuesday, b Monday is the rule in most provinci towns. It is always advisable to chec opening days and times in advance. nominal entrance fee is usual.

Most shops are closed on Sundays an Mondays (food shops and bakers ofte open for an hour or so on Sunday mor ings). Opening times vary, but 0900 unusually late. Department and cha stores will be closed by 1830; independe shops usually remain open much late Outside the large towns most close fro 1200 to 1330. Most shops are closed c public holidays (see p. 27).

Theatres usually close one day a wee but have a matinee on Sunday afternoo Cinemas are open seven days a week fro 1400 to midnight. Most have separa shows and do not run continuously.

Tipping In the majority of cafés an restaurants the price slip or bill will in clude the service charge, bearing th words *Inc. Service* or *Service Compris* wi the percentage charged. Establishmen which do not include the service char usually display a notice *Service N Compris*. In this case, an extra sum of 1 to 15 percent should be added. It customary in any case to leave any sma coins given in the change.

In hotels there will almost invariably a service charge added to the bill. It however, customary to give a small tip the porter and chambermaid in return f personal services.

Taxi drivers expect 15 to 20 percent the fare as a tip. Railway and airpo porters charge a fixed tariff per piece. T prevailing charge, varying from town town, is displayed at the platform landing bay exits.

Guides who take visitors around mon ments and museums keep a box near th exit or stand expectantly there. The should receive 1F–2F per visitor. Lavato attendants are given the odd small coins one's pocket or purse – certainly not le than 50 centimes.

Shopping The best buys in France, bo as regards quality and cost, are potter decorative glass; articles of clothing ma from silk; lace, gloves, shoes, costun jewellery; cooking utensils, domestic ele trical equipment such as blenders an toasters; wines, aperitifs, brandy, pe fumes and luxury foods. Even when th value of these purchases exceeds the co cessions granted by the customs auth rities, the value can still be of person advantage.

KEY WORDS

airport	aéroport (m)
aquarium	aquarium (m)
baker's shop	boulangerie (f)
beach	plage (f)
bishop's palace	évêché (m)
bridge	pont (m)
bus station	gare d'autobus (f)
butcher's shop	boucherie (f)
cake shop	pâtisserie (f)
camp site	terrain de camping (m)
casino	casino (m)
castle	château (m)
cathedral	cathédrale (f)
chapel	chapelle (f)
chemist's shop	pharmacie (f)
church	église (f)
convent	couvent (m)
dairy	crémerie (f)
delicatessen	
pork butcher	charcuterie (f)
farm	ferme (f)
ferry	bateau de passage (m)
fountain	source (f)
gardens	jardins public (m)
greengrocer	marchand de légumes
fresh produce shop	
hospital	hôpital (m)
hotel	hôtel (m)
house	maison (f)
inn	auberge (f)
library	bibliothèque (f)
market	marché (m)
monastery	monastère (m)
motel	motel (m)
museum	musée (m)
palace	palais (m)
park	parc (m)
petrol/gasoline	essence (f)
petrol/gas station	station-service (f)
picture gallery	musée (m)
police station	commissariat de police (m)
post office	bureau de poste (m)
racecourse	champ de courses (m)
railway station	gare (f)
skating rink	patinoire (f)
spring (spa)	source minérale (f)
square	place (f)
supermarket	supermarché (m)
swimming pool	piscine (f)
telephone	téléphone (m)
theatre	théâtre (m)
tobacconist's shop	bureau de tabac (m)
tourist information	office de tourisme (m)
	Syndicat d'Initiative (m)
Town Hall	Hôtel de Ville (m)
university	université
zoo	zoo (m)

METRIC CONVERSIONS

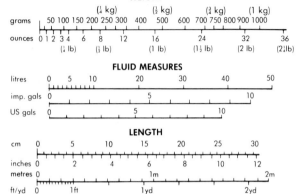

WEIGHT

FLUID MEASURES

LENGTH

DISTANCE

USEFUL ADDRESSES

French Government Tourist Offices
178 Piccadilly, London W1V 0AL (01 499 6911); 610 Fifth Avenue, New York NY 10020; 645 North Michigan Avenue, Chicago Ill. 60611; World Trade Center, No. 103 2050, Dallas, Texas 75258 (PO Box 58610); 9401 Wilshire Boulevard, Beverly Hills, Calif. 90212; Suite 610, 372 Bay Street, Toronto M5H 2W9, Ontario; 1840 Ouest, Rue Sherbrooke, Montreal H3H 1E4, Quebec.

British Consulates Societé Basque Auto, Allées Paulmy, Biarritz (25 19 58); 15 Cours de Verdun, Bordeaux (52 28 35); c/o British Rail, Gare Maritime, Boulogne (31 58 17); 9–11 rue Felix-Cadras, Calais (34 45 48); 8 rue Louis Philippe, Cherbourg (53 14 46); 11 rue des Fontaines, Dieppe (84 25 70); 6 Place de l'Yser, Dunkerque (66 78 12); Avenue de Champagne, Epernay (51 31 02); 9 Quai George V, Le Havre (42 27 47); 60 Boulevard de la Liberté, Lille (57 35 49); 4th floor, 24 rue Childebert, Lyon 2me (37 59 67); 24 Avenue de Prado, Marseille (37 68 54); 23 rue du XX Corps Americain, Metz (71 08 50); 6 rue Lafayette, Nantes (71 08 50); rue Meyerbeer, Nice (87 12 81); 109 rue St Honoré, Paris 8me (260 33 06); 10 rue du Gen. Castelnau, Strasbourg (36 64 91).

American Consulates 4 rue Esprit des Lois, Bordeaux (52 65 95); 7 Quai General Sarrail, 69454 Lyon (24 68 49); 9 rue Armeny, 13006 Marseille (337833 37); 2 Avenue Gabriel, 75382 Paris (296 12 02); 15 Avenue d'Alsace, 67082 Strasbourg.

Air Services Air Commuter, Coventry Airport, Coventry (0203 304452); Air France, 158 New Bond Street, London W1Y 0AL (01 499 9511); Air Inter (represented in Britain by Air France); Air UK, Norwich Airport, Norwich, Norfolk (0279 506301); Aurigny Air, Victoria Street, St Anne's, Alderney (048 182 2886); BritAir, 158 New Bond Street, London W1Y 0AY (01 499 9511); British Airways, West London Air Terminal, Cromwell Road, London SW7 4ED (01 370 5411); British Caledonian Airways, Gatwick Airport, Horley, Surrey (01 668 9311); British Midland Airways, East Midland Airport, Derby (0332 810552); Brymon Airways, City Airport, Plymouth (0752 707023); Dan Air Services Ltd, 71 Victoria Road, Horley, Surrey (02934 5622); Jersey European Airways, Conway Street, St Helier, Jersey (0534 45661); Lucas Air, Gatwick Airport, Horley Surrey (02934 513631); Touraine Air (Air France office).

Rail Services British Rail Travel Centre, 12 Regent Street, London SW1 (personal calls); British Rail International Inc., 270 Madison Avenue, New York NY 10016 (212 679 7355); French

Railways, 179 Piccadilly, London W1V
9BA (01 409 1224), 610 Fifth Avenue,
New York, NY 10020 (212 582 2110).

Sea Ferries Brittany Ferries, Millbay
Docks, Plymouth PL1 3 EF (0752 21321),
Norman House, Albert Johnson Quay,
Portsmouth PO2 7AE (0705 27701);
Hoverlloyd, Ramsgate, Kent (0843
55555); Olau Line (UK) Ltd, Sheerness,
Kent ME12 1SN (079 56 4981); P & O
Normandy Ferries, Arundel Towers,
Portland Terrace, Southampton SO9
4AE (0703 34141); Sally Line, Sea
Harbour Parade, Ramsgate, Kent CT11
9LN; Sealink and Seaspeed Hovercraft,
52 Grosvenor Gardens, London SW1W
0AG (01 834 2345); Townsend Thoresen
Ferries, Camden Crescent, Dover, Kent
CT16 1LD (01 734 4431 and 01 437 7800).

Motoring Organizations Automobile
Association, Fanum House, Basingstoke,
Hants RG21 2EA, c/o G A Gregson &
Sons, Gare Maritime, 62200 Boulogne
(21 317 752); Royal Automobile Club,
RAC House, Lansdowne Road, Croydon
CR9 2JA (01 686 2525), 8 Place Vendôme,
75000 Paris; Royal Scottish Automobile
Club, 11 Blythswood Square, Glasgow
G2 4AG (041 221 3850); Touring Club de
France, 65 Avenue de la Grande Armée,
75782 Paris (727 89 89).

WRITING TO FRENCH ADDRESSES

The French Post Office has adopted a
numbered postal (zip) code. Each department has a two-figure number as listed
below, and this should always be included
before the name of the town or village to
insure correct delivery; there are many
communities with the same name in
France and omission of the number (and
the absence of the name of the department) can cause misdelivery of letters.

Thus 64 Biarritz identifies the town as
in the Pyrénées-Atlantiques department.
Any digits following the first two indicate
the district in the town and should be
included if known.

Zip codes 01 Ain, 02 Aisne, 03 Allier, 04
Alpes-de-Haute-Provence, 05 Hautes-
Alpes, 06 Alpes-Maritimes, 07 Ardèche,
8 Ardennes, 09 Ariège, 10 Aube, 11
Aude, 12 Aveyron, 67 Bas-Rhin, 90
Belfort, 13 Bouches-du-Rhône, 14
Calvados, 15 Cantal, 16 Charente, 17
Charente-Maritime, 18 Cher, 19 Corrèze,
2A Corse du Sud, 2B Haute Corse, 21
Côte d'Or, 22 Côtes-du-Nord, 23 Creuze,
19 Deux-Sèvres, 24 Dordogne, 25 Doubs,
6 Drôme, 91 Éssonne, 27 Eure, 28 Eure-
et-Loir, 29 Finistère, 30 Gard, 32 Gers, 33
Gironde, 68 Haut-Rhin, 31 Haute-

Garonne, 43 Haute-Loire, 52 Haute-
Marne, 70 Haute-Saône, 74 Haute-
Savoie, 87 Haute-Vienne, 65 Hautes-
Pyrénées, 92 Hauts-de-Seine, 34 Hérault,
35 Ille-et-Vilaine, 36 Indre, 37 Indre-et-
Loire, 38 Isère, 39 Jura, 40 Landes, 41
Loir-et-Cher, 42 Loire, 44 Loire-
Atlantique, 45 Loiret, 46 Lot, 47 Lot-et-
Garonne, 48 Lozère, 49 Maine-et-Loire,
50 Manche, 51 Marne, 53 Mayenne, 54
Meurthe-et-Moselle, 55 Meuse, 56
Morbihan, 57 Moselle, 58 Nièvre, 59
Nord, 60 Oise, 61 Orne, 75 Paris, 62
Pas-de-Calais, 63 Puy-de-Dôme, 64
Pyrénées-Atlantiques, 66 Pyrénées-
Orientales, 69 Rhône, 71 Saône-et-Loire,
72 Sarthe, 73 Savoie, 77 Seine-et-Marne,
76 Seine-Maritime, 93 Seine-St-Denis,
80 Somme, 81 Tarn, 82 Tarn-et-
Garonne, 94 Val-de-Marne, 95 Val-
d'Oise, 83 Var, 84 Vaucluse, 85 Vendée,
86 Vienne, 88 Vosges, 89 Yonne, 78
Yvelines.

FESTIVALS AND PUBLIC HOLIDAYS

National Festivals and Fairs
February (mid-month), international toy
fair – Paris; March (first two weeks),
international trade fair – Nice; March (last
week), international trade fair – Lyon;
April (last week), international TV programme festival – Cannes; May (first two
weeks), international trade fair – Paris;
May (after first week), international film
festival – Cannes; May (last week), international trade fair – Bordeaux; June (last
week), aeronautics and space exhibition –
Toulouse; June (last week till early July),
Tour de France cycle race; July 14, open
air dancing and firework displays in all
towns and villages; July (mid month)
international jazz festival – Antibes;
August 15, national pilgrimage – Lourdes;
September (last week), international trade
fair – Marseille; October (alternate years),
motor show – Paris; December 24, concerts and choir singing during last hours
of Christmas Eve in most cathedrals and
churches; folk singing and dancing in
villages.

National Holidays
January 1 – New Year's Day; Easter
Monday; May 1 – Labour Day; May 8 –
VE Day; Ascension Day; Whit Monday;
July 14 – Bastille Day; August 15 – Feast
of Assumption; November 1 – All Saints'
Day; November 11 – Remembrance Day;
December 25 – Christmas Day. If any
national holiday falls on a Tuesday or a
Friday, the day between it and the nearest
Sunday is also a holiday.

PARIS

The numbers in brackets (below) are also located on the maps: (1)–(12) pp. 30–1 and (13)–(19) pp. 34–5.

Paris is served by three airports. Visitors who land at Charles de Gaulle (Roissy) or Le Bourget airports, reach the city from the north, with a view of hilly Montmartre on the right. From Orly airport, south of Paris, the bus or cab runs through Montparnasse, favoured by artists, writers and scholars. Air terminals are situated at Porte Maillot, north west of the Arc de Triomphe, and Les Invalides, near the Tour Eiffel.

Train passengers are taken close to the centre. The Gare du Nord is just outside the business section and the ancient town beside the Seine; Gare St Lazare lies near Place de la Concorde; Gare Montparnasse, on the left bank, is beside the Tour Montparnasse shopping centre.

Motorists making for central and southern France may be tempted to miss seeing Paris because of the problems of driving in a large city. In fact, the system of wide boulevards and the many new roads, all well signposted, make it reasonably easy to navigate without mishap. The best policy is to avoid arriving during rush hours (0730–0900 and 1700–1900), and to bear in mind that, as you reach the first suburban roads, ahead lies the Boulevard Périphérique which runs round the 'edge' of the city (see map pp. 30–1).

The city of Paris is divided into 20 *arrondissements* (districts). The sequence, shown on pp. 30–1, forms a clockwise spiral, and the system of numbering is quite straightforward: 1er *premier* (first), 2e *deuxième* (second), *etc.* 1er is at the very centre of Paris (Palais du Louvre, Jardin des Tuileries); 2e to the north east (Bourse); 3e to the east (Place de la République (4)); 4e to the south (Hôtel de Ville, Notre Dame (18)); 5e south across the Seine (Sorbonne (8), Panthéon (9)); 6e to the west (Palais du Luxembourg (6)); 7e to the west (government offices, Tour Eiffel); 8e north across the Seine (Champs-Élysées); 9e north east (Opéra).

The spiral continues outwards. 10e is north of 2e and 3e *arrondissements* (Gare du Nord and Gare de l'Est (3)); 11e to the south east is followed by 12e to the south extending to the banks of the Seine as the river turns south east. 13e, 14e and 15e cover the southern outer zones bounded on the west by the Seine as it curves south. North of the river comes 16e (Bois de Boulogne on one side and Arc de Triomphe to the north east); 17e covers the north-west inner suburbs; 18e includes Montmartre (2); 19e and 20e complete the spiral on the north and east.

Bearing this spiral in mind, it is always possible to reach the centre of the city from any starting point.

A good way to get your bearings is to use the vantage points. Look over the heart of Paris from the top of the south tower of Notre Dame cathedral (69m/226ft). From the top of the Arc de Triomphe (51m/164ft) there is a magnificent view of the twelve avenues radiating from l'Étoile (officially Place Charles de Gaulle but most Parisians still call it l'Étoile). The top platform of the Tour Eiffel (307m/1007ft) provides a panoramic view up to a distance of 70km/43mi on a clear day; the lower platforms overlook the entire city. In contrast the Pont des Arts, the footbridge across the Seine opposite the Palais du Louvre, presents a worm's eye view of the city's most historic and lovely buildings.

Vying with these man-made lookouts, a natural vantage point is the hill on which

Île de la Cité

Montmartre (2) stands. Rising steeply on the northern limits of the city, it gives a vista over all Paris and for 40km/25mi beyond. There is a funicular for those who shrink from the precipitous climb.

Eating and drinking locally Day and night, by road, rail and air, loads of food and drink pour into Paris from every part of France. Consequently it is impossible to describe a typically Parisian dish –

Street café, the Champs-Élysées

almost every French delicacy is to be had in the 10,000 restaurants in the capital and its surrounding area.

For the more adventurous (and less wealthy) there are restaurants serving the national dishes of every country. North African cafés and restaurants are nowadays the most numerous among these foreign establishments: the food is spicy and something of an acquired taste. European restaurants are good, especially Hungarian and Greek ones. Asiatic meals are authentic, particularly those at Indonesian and Vietnamese establishments.

A dinner in Paris can, of course, be fabulously expensive. But with the great number and variety of eating places, ranging from the small family bistro and spacious brasserie to the large self-service bars and cafés which have sprung up everywhere, a meal need not cost much. When price is a consideration but something good and really French is wanted, search out the small, unostentatious café or restaurant, in a side street close to the fashionable and busy thoroughfares, where the owner displays a handwritten notice headed *plat du jour*.

Festivals and Events (*La Semaine*, a weekly diary of events, is on sale at newsstands.) February: fashion shows. March: Prix du Président de la République at Longchamp racecourse, Bois de Boulogne. April: spring music festival. May: start of *Son et Lumière* season (to Oct.); Paris marathon (mid May); international tennis (end May to early June); Air Show (end May to June). June: Marais festival of drama, opera, music. July: Bastille Day celebrations (14 July); Esteval Festival of classical music (to mid Sept.). September: festival of contemporary art (end Sept. to Oct.); dance festival (to Nov.); Paris and Île de France autumn festival (to Dec.). October: Prix de l'Arc de Triomphe at Longchamp racecourse; Motor Show (first two weeks); jazz festival (end Oct. to Nov.).

Paris

(Pop. 2.3 million, Île-de-France 9.8 million) Although most buildings are within easy walking distance of the heart of the city, it is wise to take advantage of the excellent transport services. On your first day, a visit to the central tourist office, Office du Tourisme, 127 Champs-Élysées (open 0900–2200, closing at 1800 Sundays, holidays and out of season), will provide street maps, guides to restaurants, daily events, *etc.*

The cheapest and fastest way to get round Paris is by underground (Métro). All stations served direct are listed on panels in stations and on platforms; diagrams show the interchange stations. The RER (Réseau Express Régional) runs express trains on three separate routes, mainly serving the suburbs or going across the city.

One standard-price Métro ticket covers any distance inside the city (not on RER). Keep your ticket to show for inspection. Métro tickets can also be used on the buses and it saves time and money to buy a booklet (*carnet*) of ten. Bus routes are divided into stages (*sections*): one ticket covers two stages, two tickets cover three or more stages. Passes for two, four or seven days allow unlimited travel on Métro, RER and bus. Tickets, *carnets* and passes are sold at most Métro or bus stations and main-line terminals.

The bus is a good way of getting to know Paris. Travel is inevitably slow at rush hours, although there are bus lanes in some streets to ease the flow of traffic. Route nos. and itineraries are displayed in bus shelters and at most stops. Best routes for sightseeing start from: Gare St Lazare, bus nos. 21, 24, 29; Gare de l'Est (3), bus nos. 32, 38; Gare du Nord, bus nos. 42, 47; Hôtel de Ville, near Notre Dame, bus nos. 58, 72. (Route nos. are different on Sundays and public holidays: Gare St Lazare, 20, 21, 26, 27; Gare de l'Est, 31; Gare du Nord, 46; Gare Montparnasse, 91, 92, 95, 96.)

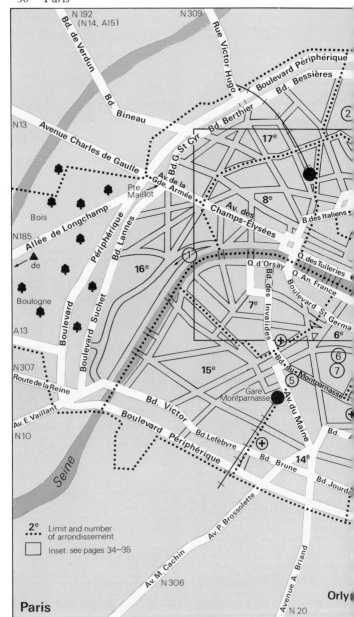

Paris

2ᵉ ···· Limit and number
of arrondissement

☐ Inset: see pages 34–35

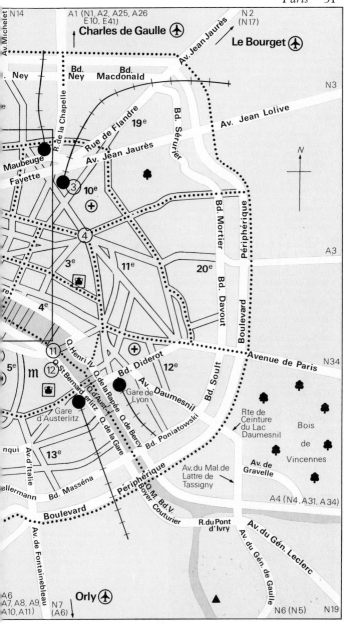

Sightseeing coach tours (booking advised) start from 214 rue de Rivoli and 4 Place des Pyramides.

There are more than 14,000 taxis on ranks or cruising the city streets. Rates are shown inside each cab. Increased rates operate between 2200–0630. There is an extra charge for trips to or from airports and main-line terminals. Maximum number of adult passengers is three. Usual tip is 15 percent of the fare shown on the meter.

Whole libraries are needed to describe the sights of Paris adequately. Here only the highlights can be briefly mentioned. They are grouped together so that each excursion involves the minimum of travel and walking.

Most museums and national monuments are closed Tuesdays and public holidays. Some museums are free, or cheaper, on Sundays. It is advisable to check details and days and times of opening in advance of a visit.

I. The heart of Paris is the **Île de la Cité**, formed by two branches of the Seine. A general view is best obtained from **Pont Neuf** (13): Métro Pont Neuf. The islet is shaped like a ship, and at the prow stands the statue of Henri IV, perhaps France's best-loved monarch, in a pretty little garden. Walking along the **Quai de l'Horloge** (14) brings you to the mass of the Conciergerie, Palais de Justice (16) and Sainte Chapelle.

This is the oldest part of Paris, site of Roman military headquarters and where the ancient Counts of Paris resisted Norman assailants. Tucked into the complex of buildings, with its tapering spire rising above, is an architectural gem: **Sainte Chapelle** (17), built in the 13th century by the devout Louis IX as a jewelled casket in stone to hold religious relics. The **Conciergerie** (15) contains the prison cells where Marie Antoinette and many aristocrats awaited the tumbrels to take them to the guillotine.

A short stroll through little streets full of interesting houses, and the façade of

Notre Dame, floodlit

Notre Dame (18) looms before you. A Druid and a Roman temple stood on this site, replaced in their turn by several Christian churches until, in 1163, the foundations of the cathedral were laid, perhaps the finest example of Gothic art in existence. There are conducted tours of the interior.

Behind Notre Dame the sub-islet of **St Louis** was bridged in the 17th century, since when it has been the residential area for wealthy citizens. Many famous artists and writers, including Corot and Baudelaire, lived at 17 **Quai d'Anjou** (19).

Crossing to the left bank (*rive gauche*) a the **Pont de Sully** (11), a wide road bears right. This is the **Boulevard St Germain**. Two minutes' walk to the left brings you to the **Jardin des Plantes** (12), 28 hectares/70 acres of gardens with botanical, herbal and pharmaceutical sections, a small zoo, and natural history museum.

Behind the Boulevard St Germain, to the left, lies **St Etienne du Mont** (10), a large church of the 15th–17th centuries in the Place Ste Geneviève, and close by lies the **Panthéon** (9), built on the site where Ste Geneviève (patron saint of Paris) was buried. Since the Revolution the Panthéon has been the resting place of France's great men.

To the north west the presence of innumerable students, bookshops and inexpensive cafés indicates that this is the area of the **Sorbonne** (8), principal university of France. North, across rue des Écoles, is the **Musée de Cluny** with medieval arts and crafts. The wide road running at right angles (back to the Seine) is the famous Boul' Mich (**Boulevard St Michel**) of the Latin Quarter. West of the boulevard lies the **Jardin du Luxembourg** (7), a pleasant resting place, with the **Palais du Luxembourg** (6) at the north end. The striking building, south west of the gardens, is the 59 storey **Tour Montparnasse**, a commercial and shopping centre with a panoramic view far into the Île-de-France.

Back down the Boulevard St Michel towards the Île de la Cité, the starting point of the tour lies beyond the Place St Michel.

II. From the same starting point the attractions of the right bank (*rive droite*) will involve more time though not so much walking or transport from place to place. Standing on the Pont Neuf and facing away from Notre Dame, the **Palais du Louvre**, to the right, runs along the river bank. This is the largest town palace in the world: once the brain and heart of the nation, with the royal residence, the

Palais du Louvre

military headquarters, the treasure house and the government offices under a series of roofs. It was a formidable place as early as 1200 and a storehouse of works of art by 1500. It has been said that one could take up residence in this 'Queen of Museums' and fail to exhaust its treasures in a lifetime. Certainly it is exasperating when time demands that a visit be restricted to seeing only a few of the treasures, such as the *Mona Lisa* and the *Venus de Milo*. But the authorities arrange a variety of tours which cover items of special interest and different periods of time. There are seven museums: Greek and Roman antiquities, Egyptian and Oriental antiquities, painting, sculpture, art treasures, decorative arts, and (across the **Jardin des Tuileries**) the French Impressionists in the **Musée du Jeu de Paume**.

This brings you to the **Place de la Concorde**, an immense square each side of which 250m/273yds long. When it was laid out in 1757 it was surrounded by a moat. This was the place where Louis XVI, Marie Antoinette and many hundreds of aristocrats were executed during the Revolution.

To the left, across the wide bridge over the Seine, can be seen the **Palais Bourbon**, the French 'House of Commons'.

Looming beyond this building, and approached by magnificent formal gardens, is the **Hôtel des Invalides** (*Son et Lumière* shows, evenings May–Oct.), so called because Louis XIV built it as a home for wounded soldiers. It is an enormous place, with 16km/10mi of corridors; only part of it is open to visitors because it is a military administration centre. The huge dome seen as one approaches, is over the **Église du Dôme**, built as part of the hospital. It contains the tomb of Napoleon. Across the Boulevard des Invalides is the **Musée Rodin** with works by the sculptor and paintings by Monet, Renoir and Van Gogh.

Retrace your steps back to Église du Dôme on Av. de Tourville, ahead lies the **Champ de Mars** with the **Tour Eiffel** at the far end. Those who cannot face the thought of taking the lift to the top

(307m/1007ft) will find wonderful views from the lower landings.

Across the river the modern building is the **Palais de Chaillot** (1), built for an exhibition in 1937. It houses museums devoted to mankind, ships, architecture and the cinema. A walk along the riverside takes you back to Île de la Cité. But for the visitor who still has some time there could be a restful trip on a *bateau mouche* moored on the right bank beside Pont d'Iéna.

III. The two previous tours have covered all the major sights within a short distance of the Île de la Cité. The third begins at the Place de la Concorde. Walking a short distance along the right bank of the Seine brings you to two palaces, the **Petit Palais** and the **Grand Palais**. The large one houses France's major exhibitions, notably the motor show; the smaller is an interesting fine arts and science museum and also runs a series of temporary art exhibitions. Turning right behind these buildings brings you to the **Champs-Élysées**, laid out in the 17th century, and, despite its length, the perfect thoroughfare to follow on foot, with its smart shops, cinemas, and the cafés where one can sit and watch the world pass by. At the top stands the **Arc de Triomphe** in the **Place Charles de Gaulle** (formerly

Arc de Triomphe

l'Étoile), constructed over a period of 20 years to commemorate the glory of Imperial France and Napoleon's victories.

After negotiating the swirling traffic to reach the island on which the arch stands, you can take the lift (1000–1800, summer; to dusk, winter; closed public holidays) to the top from which there is a splendid view of Paris; note the small replica of the arch about 3km/1¾mi away in the gardens of the Palais du Louvre. Protected by the arch is the grave of France's **Unknown Soldier**, the flame of remembrance burning before it. The ceremony of rekindling the flame takes place on days of historical importance.

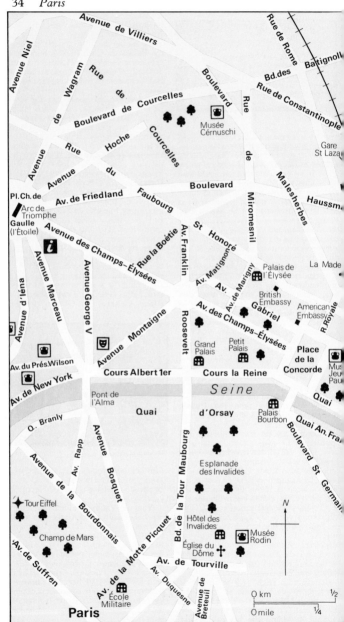

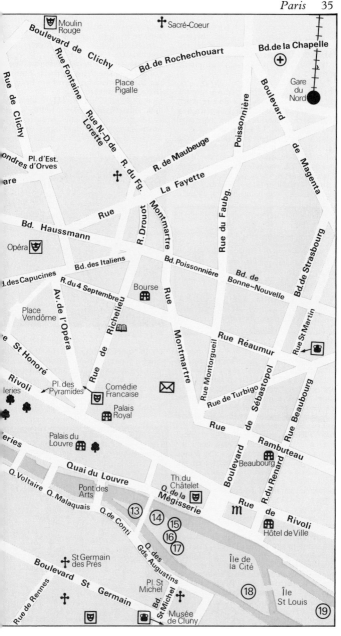

North west of the arch, down the Av. de la Grande Armée, is the modern International Centre, dominated by the **Palais des Congrès**, a towering building comprising hotel, restaurants and trading suites.

Retracing one's steps down the Champs-Élysées, halfway down on the left the first wide road (**La Boétie**) leads to an intersection with **rue du Faubourg St Honoré**, a famous street of expensive shops. **Palais de l'Élysée**, official residence of the President of France, is on the right. To the left, at the end of this street, is **La Madeleine** (Church of St Mary Magdalene). It was being built as a church when Napoleon rose to power. He turned it into a Temple of Glory. Not until 1842 was it finally consecrated as a church.

Boulevard des Capucines (Opéra)

Beyond it stands the **Opéra** on the **Boulevard des Capucines**, leading to the ancient gates of Paris and now a very popular shopping zone. The Opéra is the largest live theatre in the world, opulent in marble and red and gold décor.

In this area, crammed with cafés, shops, and places of entertainment as far as the **rue de Rivoli**, are some notable places of interest. Across the boulevard from the Opéra and bearing right is the **Place Vendôme**, offering a peaceful contrast. The area was cleared to provide a setting for a statue of Louis XIV. The revolutionaries got rid of the statue and put up a figure of Liberty. Napoleon celebrated his victory at Austerlitz by erecting a monument in imitation of the Trajan column in Rome.

Turning left along the **rue St Honoré** you come to the **Palais Royal**, built by Richelieu, and the home of Queen Henrietta of England when she was exiled under the Commonwealth. Farther on, to the left across the Boulevard de Sébastopol, the Centre National d'Art et de Culture (Pompidou Centre, also known as **Beaubourg**) merits at least half a day to itself: exhibition halls, modern art gallery, concert hall, a galaxy of sideshows and, at the top, reached by an exterior transparent escalator, a café and restaurant.

These tours cover only the most essential sights at the centre of Paris. There is one further area which must not be omitted: **Montmartre** (2) to the north. Routes 4 and 12 on the Métro serve the area. The Place Pigalle, Moulin Rouge and Boulevard de Clichy are names synonymous with the 'bright lights' of Paris, and the area is also rich in history, espe-

Place Pigalle

cially **Sacré-Coeur** (the Basilica of the Sacred Heart), built by national subscription as a symbol of hope after the Franco-Prussian war of 1870–71, contrasting with the 12th-century church of St Pierre just behind it. *Boulogne 242km/150mi, Calais 292/181, Le Havre 204/127.*

Sacré-Coeur

BRITTANY AND NORMANDY

The north and north-west coastline of Brittany offers a great variety of scenery, with scores of resorts, mostly small and unspoiled, appealing to those who prefer a quiet but interesting holiday without too much heat in high summer.

Brittany is the promontory of Europe, thrusting out into the Atlantic between Nantes and the headland north of Brest, then curving on a less rugged coast facing the entrance to the Channel as far as the impressive Mont-St-Michel. The cliffs, headlands and crags on the west coast are mostly of pink or purple granite; they protect many beaches of fine sand, and, despite the obvious effect of wind and waves, the climate is mild, thanks to the Gulf Stream. The Bretons are a maritime people, proud of their individuality, and wherever the coast provides shelter there is a fishing village, only a few – such as Brest, Lorient and St-Nazaire – showing much trace of modern development.

Inland Brittany, known in Breton as L'Argoat (land of woods), is too often ignored by tourists rushing to the coast. The whole land was once covered with impenetrable forests of oak and beech. Woods still remain among the tiny farms, and stretches of uncultivated land covered with broom and heather survive. The interior is dominated by the 'mountains', so-called not because of their height but on account of their wild and rugged appearance, giving spectacular views over the whole region.

Brittany is an ancient land, where the Celtic tribes settled before moving on to Britain. Prehistoric sites abound, and history since those remote times can be traced from megalithic circles through early Christian monuments in the unique parish *closes* (built round cemeteries) to the cathedrals and imposing castles of the Middle Ages.

As one moves east from the borders of Brittany, the Normandy coast is made up of high cliffs interspersed with good beaches and resorts which occupy every attractive site. The Cotentin Peninsula, in which Cherbourg stands, is reminiscent of the wild coast of Brittany – the rock-strewn sea's edge and tidal races are awesome even in serene weather. Between the peninsula and Le Havre the low cliffs made this stretch of coast the choice for the Allied invasion in 1944. Now it is a place of quiet family resorts, with Deauville and Trouville retaining their stylish appeal which emerged at the turn of the century. Further east the cliffs rise again and towns are few as far as Dieppe.

Inland, perhaps the most striking features are the numerous rivers and the lush farmlands which border them. The country is well-wooded and there are few hills. For those interested in the arts and buildings the interior of Normandy offers an almost inexhaustible source of study. More than 50 churches and abbeys are listed as of exceptional importance, with the cathedrals of Bayeux, Coutances, Évreux, Lisieux and Rouen unsurpassed in historic interest and beauty.

Crêpes and Calvados No vistor to the Breton coast can remain ignorant of the fact that this is one of the best areas for shellfish in all France. Cooked or raw, these delicacies are served in great variety and always in quantity, the dishes frequently including marine creatures the stranger cannot identify. No need for forebodings beyond the danger of over-indulgence. Great care is taken to harvest the 'fruits of the sea' from unpolluted waters. Freshwater fish – perch, pike and salmon – are a speciality inland.

For children and those wary of novel foods, the places to patronize at any time of the day are the little cafés called *crêperies*. They serve sweet or savoury *crêpes* (pancakes cooked on a griddle) which are inexpensive and nutritious. Fillings can be of meat, fish or cheese, and the sweet versions have all sorts of fruits and sugary confections.

A more robust meal can include salt-marsh mutton served with white beans, or tripe simmered in cider – both comforting if the day is a little chilly.

The most usual wine offered is Muscadet. There are several unusual liqueurs, of which strawberry liqueur is

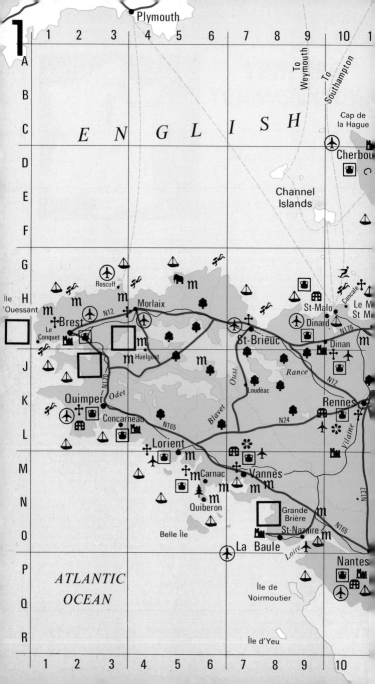

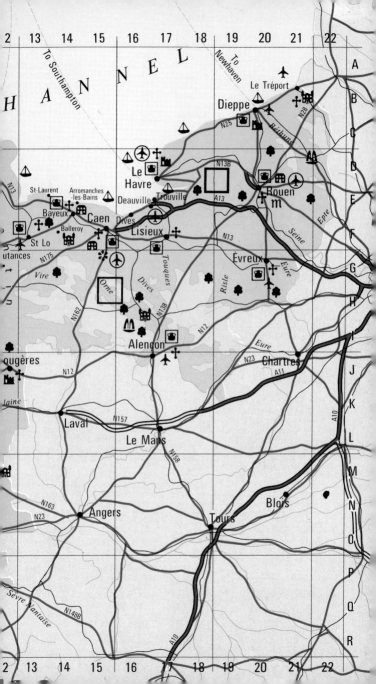

among the best. Old-fashioned bars can offer Chouchenn, a type of mead.

Normandy shares with Brittany many of the local foods, notably *crêpes* and salt-marsh mutton. The province is the great dairy centre of France, and cream and butter are used lavishly in scores of dishes. Highly recommended local dishes are Caen tripe and Mont-St-Michel omelettes. And don't forget those two superb cheeses Camembert and Pont l'Evèque.

Cider is produced – and drunk – in vast quantities in Normandy. It can be deceptively strong. Calvados (apple brandy) should not be missed as an aperitif or after-dinner luxury – but it is definitely a 'drink but don't drive' liqueur.

Festivals and Events The Breton Pardons (religious festivals), with pilgrims in festive costume, take place in almost every town and village ·in the province during the summer and autumn. The most colourful are at Tréguier (19 May), St-Brieuc (31 May), Guingamp (first Saturday in July), Locronan (second Sunday in July), Quimper (mid-July), Roscoff (third Sunday in July), Ste-Anne-d'Auray (26 July), Perros-Guirec (15 August), Josselin (8 September), Carnac (10–13 September). Eastertide, carnival and drama – Deauville, Trouville. Whit Monday, fête – Quimperlé. June 5–6, D-day anniversary celebrations in Normandy coast towns. June (first week), regatta – Cherbourg. July (first week), amateur film festival – St-Cast. July 11, embroiderers' festival – Pont-l'Abbé. July (mid-month), drama festival – St-Malo. July (third Sunday), carnation festival – Paramé, St-Malo. July (last week), pilgrimage across sands – Mont-St-Michel. August (first Sunday), gorse festival – Pont Aven. August (first week), international bagpipe festival – Brest. August (early), international Celtic festival – Lorient. August (third Sunday), fishermen's festival – Concarneau. September-October, horse racing and parades – Le Pin-au-Haras. September (first week), US film festival – Deauville. September (second weekend), folklore festival – St-Brieuc. September (mid-month), horse and dog show (which dates back 1000 years) – Lessay. October 3, national pilgrimage – Lisieux.

Atlantic coast, near La Baule

Alençon   J17

Orne (pop. 35,000) Alençon stands on a main road (N12) from Paris to the Normandy coast. The town was severely damaged during the liberation of France in 1944, but fortunately the finest buildings were of granite and have been almost perfectly restored. The Gothic church of Notre Dame has some beautiful 16th-century stained glass. Two museums deserve to be more popular than they are one, in the Hôtel de Ville, has a fine collection of lace and pictures by Normandy artists; the other, the 15th-century Maison d'Ozé, Place de la Madeleine, has works by Watteau, Poussin and Fragonard, and also one of the finest collections of French lace in the world. Alençon lace, still a cottage industry, was originally reserved for the exclusive use of the Queens of France. There are many stud farms in the district, including one run by the state at **Le Haras du Pin** (40km/25mi north through Sées on the N138). The stabling and farm buildings were designed by Hardouin-Mansart who built Versailles. Some 200 of the finest stallions in France are kept here – Percheron draught horses, racehorses and trotting horses. Visitors are allowed to visit the stables and exercise grounds. *Le Mans 49km/30mi, Rouen 144/89.*

Arromanches-les-Bains E14

Calvados This town was known only to few discerning French families who loved its immense sandy beach before the invasion of 1944 put the name into history. Here, on June 6, 1944, the Allied armies landed from 4000 ships and 1000 small craft. The remains of the Mulberry floating harbour are still in position, and in the Invasion Museum is a diorama of the landings with a recorded commentary in English. Apart from its wartime associations, Arromanches is a charming resort with pretty, modern houses and many new, small hotels. This stretch of invasion coast, now called the Mother-of-Pearl Coast, has a number of unpretentious resorts which are ideal for families with children. To the east is **Ouistreham** (27km/17mi), a yachting centre. Thereafter the D514 hugs the coast to Arromanches, passing **Riva Bella**, **Langrune** (with associations back to the days of invading Norsemen), **St-Aubin** and **Courseulles**. To the west of Arromanches is the fishing port of **Port-en-Bessin**, planned in the 17th century as a naval base, and then the villages of **St Laurent** and **Vierville** which mark the stretch of the coast known as Omaha Beach, along which the American forces fought to get a foothold. There is a cemetery and memorial here to the 1st and

29th US divisions and the 5th Eng. Special Brigade. *Bayeux 10km/6mi, Caen 27/17.*

La Baule   O8

Loire-Atl (pop. 15,000) This is one of the most fashionable resorts on the Atlantic coast. The sandy beach, facing south, stretches for 8km/5mi in a gentle curve and is protected by pine woods planted to fix the shifting sand and shelter the town from the north winds. These woods, with the promontories of Penchâteau and Chemoulin at either end, ensure a mild climate in summer and winter. There are scores of hotels ranging from the luxurious to the modest and inexpensive family establishment. Chalets, flats and studio apartments are available in quantity for renting, the French moving to this resort for long summer periods. In all hotels and restaurants (the most expensive being near the casino) fish dishes are outstanding. All around La Baule are unspoiled Breton villages. Of special interest is **Batz**, 10km/6mi west along the D99, where Balzac lived. Its church has a 60m/200ft tower, with a magnificent panorama of sea, coastline, and hinterland from the top. 5km/3mi inland, on the D774, is **Guérande**, a medieval town with its walls, towers and gates almost intact, and part of its moat still water-filled. The castle is partially ruined, but one section houses a museum of old Breton furniture and local costumes. *Nantes 78km/48mi, Vannes 72/45.*

Bayeux   E14

Calvados (pop. 14,000) Despite its situation close to the invasion area of 1944, Bayeux largely escaped damage. The town has existed for nearly 2000 years, at first as a Viking settlement to which the Dukes of Normandy used to send their sons for education in the Norse language, seamanship, and the arts of war. The streets are twisted, bringing surprising scenes at every turn. A photographer's dream is the rue Bourbesneur, full of ancient houses, one with a stair turret to a watchroom. Another street with beautiful medieval buildings is the rue des Cuisiniers. All the streets lead to the focal point of Bayeux, the cathedral of Notre Dame, a huge building for such a small town and reminiscent of Norman Gothic in England, for which indeed it served as a model. In the adjoining museum is the Bayeux Tapestry, an extraordinarily vivid 'strip cartoon' with 58 scenes of the Norman Conquest of 1066. Measuring 70m/230ft in length, the hanging was possibly embroidered in Kent at the order of the Conqueror's half-brother, Bishop Cdo. Multilanguage commentaries are transmitted to explain the story to visitors. West of the town the road splits into the N13 running direct to Cherbourg (92km/57mi), and the N172, D73, D13, D8 and N174 which detours for an additional 16km/10mi through two outstanding Normandy towns. **Balleroy** nestles in a semicircle round its château, one of the finest in France, and built by François Mansart who was Louis XIV's master architect. The interior is beautifully furnished, mostly with 17th- and 18th-century furniture, and has many priceless works of art. A modern attraction is the balloon museum developed by a US society. **Cérisy**, 8km/5mi farther, is not notable until one visits the adjacent woods, hidden in which is an abbey of a perfection which makes the finest Gothic pale by comparison. It was founded by the father of William the Conqueror. *Caen 27km/17mi.*

Brest   I2

Finistère (pop. 172,000) Brest, almost completely destroyed during the war, is a show place of reconstruction as a modern town, retaining its traditional character and its history. One of France's largest naval bases, Brest belongs to the workaday world rather than to holidays, but its situation makes it an excellent base for Brittany, not least because of its wide variety of hotels, moderately priced for the discerning French and with high standards of cuisine. Brest has one of the largest roadsteads in Europe, a wonderful sight from the Cours Dajot. The ancient castle and the old ramparts are of interest; some parts of the arsenal and dockyard, however, are open only to French citizens. There are small beaches near the town at **Porsmilin** and **Le Trez-Hir** along the D789, and beyond them stands the hamlet of **St-Mathieu**. Its abbey church is in ruins, battered by the winds of this ocean-washed headland. The island of **Ouessant** (Ushant) can be seen from the lighthouse. Boat trips to Ouessant leave from Brest and from Le Conquet, just north of St-Mathieu. The trip takes about three hours and can be rough. The island has some 1500 inhabitants who fish, tend sheep and manage to grow figs against the stone walls of their gardens. *Nantes 302km/187mi, Paris 580/360.*

Caen   F15

Calvados (pop. 123,000) Caen, which was savagely bombarded in 1944, still merits the description of 'the city of spires'. The Normans built well, and the church towers stood when smaller buildings crumbled. Even the Tour de Saint-Jean, which leans well away from the perpendicular, was little damaged. Standing at the junction of the Orne and Odon

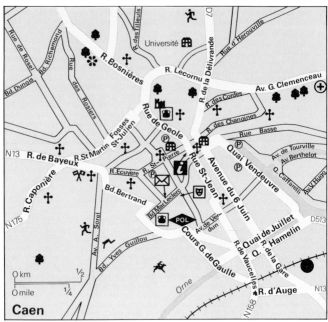

Caen

rivers, Caen has some lovely old houses bordering the water. Other notable ones are the Maison de Bois in rue St Pierre and the Hôtel d'Escoville set around a courtyard alongside the damaged church of St Pierre. Two large churches, the Abbaye aux Hommes and Abbaye aux Dames, were built on the orders of William the Conqueror and his Queen. Hotels and restaurants are centred in the newly built area, notably in the Place du Maréchal Foch and the Place de la République. Caen is famous for *tripes à la mode. Cherbourg 120km/75mi, Le Havre 106/66, Rouen 126/79.*

Cancale   H10
I-et-V (pop. 5000) This is a little fishing village which has in recent years become popular with yachtsmen and those energetic people who want to enjoy water skiing and underwater exploration. Many tiny bays make the area an expert swimmer's paradise, and the coast around the Pointe du Grouin is a fascinating riot of rocks, reefs, tiny islets and creeks. From the tower of the church of Cancale is a wonderful view across the bay towards **Mont-St-Michel**, towering out of the water. Gastronomes know Cancale as the village with the best oysters in Europe.

The restaurants clustering round the little harbour are also famous for the mutton from lambs which graze on salty grass. *St-Malo 10km/6mi.*

Carnac   M6
Morbihan (pop. 3700) The name Carnac is familiar to archaeologists throughout the world. The town is at the centre of a vast area of megaliths which stretch for 24km/15mi along the coast. Among the 3000 pieces of granite which stand in carefully designed patterns are two especially famous stones: the Merchants' Table, weighing 101 tonnes/100 tons, and the Mener-Hroec'h, broken by lightning, but originally 20m/66ft high. Carnac consists of two communities. The older town has a wonderful museum containing items found in the prehistoric graves of the area. The church is dedicated to St Cornély, regarded as the patron saint of horned cattle, and two bulls are carved on the façade of the building. On the Sunday falling in mid-September the cattle are brought to the old town for the Blessing of the Beasts. The other Carnac is a modern one on the sandy beach which faces south, protected from the Atlantic swell and ocean winds by the Quiberon peninsula. *Quiberon 54km/33mi, Vannes 32/20.*

Cherbourg   D11

Manche (pop. 35,000) A terminal for Atlantic freighters and Channel ferries, Cherbourg was constructed as a haven from the currents and the winds which sweep round the Cotentin peninsula. Largely rebuilt since the war, its marine terminal gives many a tourist the first glimpse of Gallic efficiency and courtesy. Motorboat trips round this man-made port are interesting. In the Hôtel de Ville the Henry Gallery contains many pictures by Millet, who was born in the vicinity. The Fort du Roule, overlooking the harbour, is now a museum of the Second World War and the liberation of France. Too infrequently visited is the **Cap de la Hague**, to the north west of the city along the D901. Just further south the cliffs at **Nez de Jobourg**, rising to nearly 160m/520ft, are the highest in Europe. From this plateau, where there are Viking earthworks, a magnificent view over the honeycombed coast and the sea as far as the Channel Islands can be enjoyed. *Caen 120km/75mi, Paris 350/217.*

Concarneau   L3

Finistère (pop. 19,000) This Breton fishing port has become very popular with British visitors. Built on an island and surrounded by ramparts, it is one of the most picturesque centres in Brittany. The fishing here is mainly for tuna, and the unloading of the catches and the auctions provide never-ceasing interest. Ville-Close, near the main harbour, is a fortress protecting the ancient town where the English were besieged during the 14th-century wars with France. The nearby bathing beach of **Sables Blancs** is a sheltered, pretty area with villas fringing the sand. *Quimper 20km/12mi, Vannes 100/62.*

Deauville   E17

Calvados (pop. 5700) Deauville is the principal resort on the Côte Fleurie; neighbouring ones are **Trouville** and **Villers**, favoured by families; **Houlgate**, hidden in a valley of quiet lanes and pastureland; **Dives** where William the Conqueror assembled his invasion fleet (the church contains a list of nobles who

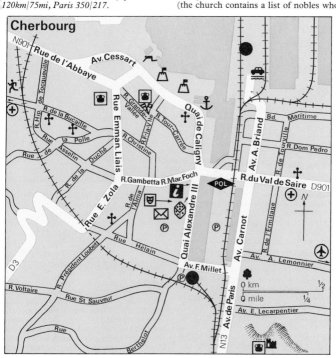

Cherbourg

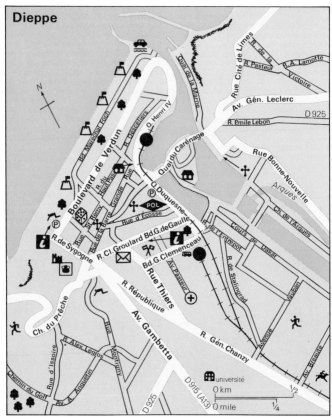

Dieppe

accompanied him in 1066); and **Cabourg**, fashionable and rather expensive. Deauville itself, separated from Trouville by a small river, has a wonderful beach with a 1½km/1mi long board walk for the fashion models, film and TV stars, and European aristocrats who get their suntan at this traditionally exclusive resort. The town's attractions include a casino, a theatre, a racecourse, a polo ground, night clubs and a huge yacht marina. Many of the most famous shops in Paris maintain boutiques around the casino. *Le Havre 72km/45mi, Paris 200/124.*

Dieppe   B20

Seine-Mar (pop. 26,000) Dieppe is not devoted solely to handling cross-Channel traffic and entertaining day trippers. It has long been popular with French families and has all the amenities of a high class resort. The beach is safe and sandy, and the town, though seriously damaged in the war, has many places of historical interest. Within the 15th-century castle is a museum of navigational instruments and ancient manuscripts. *Abbeville 65km/40mi, Paris 180/112, Rouen 58/36.*

Dinan   I10

C-du-Nord (pop. 16,000) Dinan stands on the River Rance just above the tidal stretch. Most of the town is high above the river, protected by huge ramparts from which there are splendid views of the river and the 14th-century castle of Duchess Anne. Fascinating little streets and squares provide a delight for the artist and photographer. Some houses are built on tilts to counteract the steep slopes. Down to the river there are terraced gardens. Two ancient churches, St Malo and St Sauveur, are typical of medieval Norman style. The municipal museum, in the keep of the castle of Duchess Anne, is devoted principally to Breton folklore. *Rennes 50km/31mi, St-Malo 25/16.*

Dinard H10

I-et-V (pop. 9500) This modern resort faces St-Malo across the wide estuary of the Rance. The central beach fringed with cafés and shops can become crowded, but there are innumerable sandy coves among the rocks facing the estuary and the Channel. There are 8km/5mi of walks along the low, undulating cliff edge from which most visitors manage to select what becomes virtually a private beach. Dinard is remarkable because its annual average temperature is considerably higher than elsewhere in Brittany, thanks to warm air currents brought by the Gulf Stream and its sheltered position on the estuary. Apart from the many places of modern entertainment, the town has a fine maritime museum and aquarium (a branch of the French National Museum of Natural History). A big attraction is a visit to the dam, artificial lake and generators of the first tidal power station in the world, (permits to visit from Syndicat d'Initiative in the town centre), about ½km/1mi up the Rance estuary. Three nights per week from June to September outdoor concerts are held under floodlights on the Promenade du Clair de Lune. *Dinan 22km/14mi.*

Évreux G20

Eure (pop. 50,000) This busy town handling the market produce of a large part of the 'larder of France', has had a stormy history for more than 2000 years – constantly assailed, sacked and burned by a succession of enemies, from the Romans, Vandals, Normans and English to the Germans in 1940. Vestiges of past glories remain: part of the cathedral built and rebuilt between the 12th and 17th centuries, and the 14th-century abbey church of St Taurin. *Caen 121km/75mi, Chartres 77/48, Le Havre 120/75.*

Le Havre D17

Seine-Mar (pop. 217,000) This town was founded in the 16th century as a major port. It was obliterated in the Second World War. But Le Havre emerged as an example of the ideal 20th-century town – a claim endorsed by an international congress of architects. The ship's passenger's first glimpse of the new city is the 14-storey Ocean Gateway. Behind it stretches the Avenue Foch, wider than the Champs-Élysées in Paris. The Museum

and House of Culture provide a glimpse of what museums in the future will be like. Le Havre's associations with Britain and the USA are many. The Quai Notre Dame commemorates the spot where Lafayette in 1779 received a sword of honour from the Congress of the United States and from which he sailed with the expedition to aid the colonists for whom his victory at Yorktown decided the independence of America. *Amiens 180km/112 mi.*

Lisieux F17

Calvados (pop. 27,000) Lisieux is largely a new town, the picturesque medieval timbered houses having been destroyed in 1944. Fortunately the Gothic cathedral and most of the relics of St Thérèse ('the Little Flower') were unharmed. At the convent where she lived for nine years a charming statuette of the saint stands at the entrance to the chapel, alongside which is a small museum devoted to her relics. Just outside the town, on a hill, stands the basilica, consecrated in 1954, the objective of pilgrims from all over the world. The chief pilgrimages take place in the last week of September, culminating in ceremonies on October 3, the anniversary of St Thérèse's canonization in 1925. *Caen 49km/30mi, Rouen 82/51.*

Lorient M5

Morbihan (pop. 72,000) In the 17th century this was the main port for trading to the Orient. In 1940–44 it was a major German U-boat base, resulting in repeated attacks which destroyed 80 percent of the town. The spacious new city is a good centre for exploring nearby fishing villages. In early August the international Celtic festival is the largest of its kind.

Mont-St-Michel I11

Manche This semi-island rock (of volcanic origin) rises abruptly between the salt marshes and an immense sandy bay of 26,000 hectares/100 sq mi. It is certainly the foremost natural wonder of France. Approached by a causeway, with ample bus and car parking space at the end of it, the mount is almost perfectly circular at the base, rising in four levels on one side, but sheer on the outer curve. The first place of worship was built on the top of the mount in 709 – a tiny chapel. In the 12th century the masterpieces seen today were begun – the church and monastic buildings of the Benedictine order. In the 15th century, fortifications were added. Napoleon turned the mount into a prison and it remained so until a little more than a century ago. The church and summit of the mount are reached by the Grande Rue, bordered at the base by restaurants, cafés and souvenir shops. The most memorable experience is to stay at Mont-St-Michel

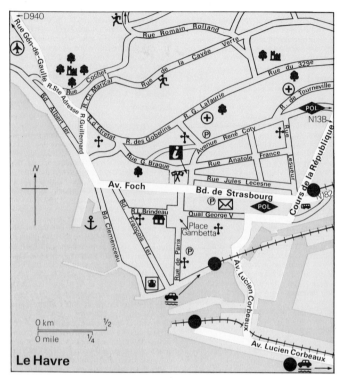

Le Havre

after the trippers have gone and the shops are closed. To watch the moon rise or the sun set over the vast bay is one of the most awesome experiences possible in Europe. The tide races in at more than 60m/65yd a minute, rising as much as 15m/49ft in periods of full moon. No one, not even on a galloping horse, could outpace the incoming sea. In any event the bay is full of quicksand; neither machine nor living animal has any chance of resisting the pull downwards. *St-Malo 60km/37mi.*

Nantes   O11
Loire-Atl (pop. 264,000) On the estuary of the Loire, Nantes is a bustling university and industrial city dominated by its great castle, once the residence of the Dukes of Britanny and notorious as the home of Gilles de Rais. Many fine merchants' houses with walled gardens overlook the river. At Belvèdère Ste Anne is a magnificent panorama of river and countryside. In the Musée des Beaux-Arts in rue Georges Clemenceau are 2000 canvases,

including works by Canaletto, Caravaggio, Rubens, Rembrandt and all well known French artists. The Musée Dobrée, Place Jean V, is housed in an old manor house and is devoted mainly to archaeology. The Museum of Decorative Art is inside the castle and has a unique collection of Breton crafts, costumes, toys and furnishings. Also in the castle is a collection of relics from ships when Nantes was a base for the slave trade between Africa and America. A new museum in rue Georges Clemenceau is devoted to Jules Verne, born in Nantes in 1828. The town is an excellent centre for both seaside resorts and the châteaux of the Loire. *Angers 90km/56mi, Rennes 106/66.*

Quiberon   N6
Morbihan (pop. 4700) Quiberon stands at the tip of the narrow tongue of land beyond Carnac. It is one of the most popular bathing resorts in southern Brittany. On the western side of the

promontory (Côte Sauvage), the Atlantic rollers ceaselessly break on rocks and into caves (bathing dangerous). On the eastern side are safe sandy beaches with pine trees to provide shade and shelter. In summer, boats leave at frequent intervals from the sardine fishers' harbour for Belle Île, an hour's trip. *Nantes 150 km/93mi.*

Quimper   K3

Finistère (pop. 60,000) Quimper is named after the Breton word for the junction of waters. The town stands at the confluence of the Steir and Odet and is a convenient centre for visiting the extreme west of France. Mont Frugy is a good vantage point for viewing the town, whose cathedral dominates the scene. Although most of the construction is 13th-century, the spires were built in 1853, but are regarded as perfect Gothic. The two museums are interesting buildings. The Breton museum near the cathedral is housed in the former bishop's palace (15th century); the Musée des Beaux Arts in the Place St-Corentin is the ancient Hôtel de Ville. The 3-day folk festival at the end of July is one of France's biggest. *Brest 79km/49mi, Rennes 206/128.*

Rennes   K11

I-et-V (pop. 210,000) Standing at the junction of the main roads between Brittany and the rest of France, Rennes is the region's principal town. Of ancient origin, most of the old town was destroyed by fire in 1720, but some medieval houses and defensive walls remain around the cathedral. Summer visitors should not miss the famous Thabor rose gardens. *Caen 173km/108mi, Nantes 106/66.*

Rouen   E20

Seine-Mar (pop. 118,000) Rouen is best approached along the Corniche road high above the Seine, where the town is spread out below the traveller in an intriguing pattern of houses, port installations, factories and towering Gothic spires. The most notable building is the cathedral of Notre Dame (late Gothic with a lantern tower of iron and bronze, 1827–77). Here was interred the heart of Richard Coeur de Lion. The building has been wonderfully reconstructed after major war damage. Two other churches among the many in Rouen of special interest are St Ouen, a Gothic masterpiece, and St Maclou, richly decorated and with magni-

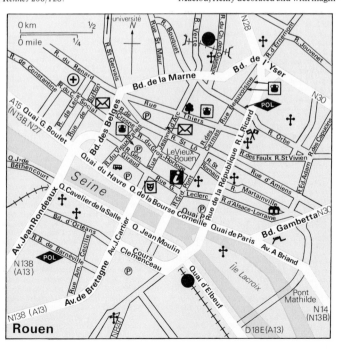

ficent wood carving. Medieval features in the old town include the Gros Horloge, a clock tower above the bustling street of the same name; and the partially restored Palais de Justice. Near the Rive Droite railway station is the house where Joan of Arc was jailed and interrogated. The exact spot where she was burned at the stake in 1431 is marked on the pavement in the Place du Vieux-Marché. The area has recently been rebuilt with a church and national monument to Joan. In the Musée des Beaux Arts are some 2000 pictures and a vast collection of ceramics. *Amiens 115km/71mi, Dieppe 56/35, Paris 135/84.*

St-Brieuc   I7

C-du-Nord (pop. 56,000) St-Brieuc is a bustling town a short distance from the sea on a plateau providing views over miles of valleys and coastline. Its authorities have done much to popularize it as a resort, and there are many hotels, restaurants and facilities for amusement. Just over 8km/5mi from the centre of the town is the **Rosaires** bathing beach. Most of the town is modern, spacious and efficient, but a medieval section remains grouped around the 12th-century cathedral. *Rennes 100km/62mi, St-Malo 76/47.*

St-Lô   F13

Manche (pop. 25,000) A popular stopping place for touring to and from Cherbourg and Brittany, this town was originally the Gaulish settlement of *Briovere* and an important trade centre from the 6th century. It was subject to prolonged and intensive attack in the summer of 1944 and almost completely destroyed. A touching memory of that time is the memorial to Major Howie of the US army. He pledged himself to be the man at the head of the town's liberating forces. He was killed during the siege, but his men bore his body in a coffin at the front of the column which first entered the town. The modern St-Lô has been carefully planned to dominate the hill on which the original community lived when protected by ramparts. Just outside the town is one of France's most famous stud farms with 250 stallions for breeding racehorses and Percherons. Visits to the stables are arranged daily. *Caen 60km/37mi, Cherbourg 78/49.*

St-Malo   H10

I-et-V (pop. 46,000) This was originally a pirates' stronghold, and appears to be anchored in the sea which surrounds it on three sides. Immensely thick walls protect the medieval town – so strong that they were little damaged by bombs or shellfire. However, the retreating German army set fire to the town in August 1944, and when the fires died down a week later the place was in ruins. By numbering the blocks of stone in the unsafe buildings and lovingly copying the medieval stonemasons, the town was reborn, and weathering has already restored the 17th-century appearance. The wide estuary of the Rance which washes the ramparts on one side is a great yachting centre. Before 1967, crossing the river to Dinard and the holiday resorts of **St-Lunaire** and **St-Briac** involved using the ferries or going as far as the bridge at Châteauneuf; the road bridge on top of the tidal dam has cut the distance between St-Malo and Dinard to 7km/4mi. *Rennes 70km/43mi.*

St-Nazaire   O9

Loire-Atl (pop. 70,000) St-Nazaire is one of the great shipbuilding centres of Europe, with two basins where France's biggest ships are built. The huge German submarine base was so strongly constructed that it still remains much as it was in the war. Much of the town has been rebuilt, with pleasant boulevards bordering the bathing beaches. North of St-Nazaire is the peaty plain of the **Grande Brière**, dotted with tiny villages and farms; this is a great centre for wild fowling, ornithology and botany. *Nantes 60km/37mi, Rennes 125/78.*

Le Tréport   B21

Seine-Mar (pop. 7000) This is the most northerly port of Normandy. Julius Caesar called it *Ulterior Portus* when it was the supply port for the Roman legions in Britain. 5km/3mi away is **Eu**, with a great château, where Queen Victoria stayed, and a Gothic church dedicated to St Lawrence – Archbishop Lawrence O'Toole of Dublin who died in the monastery in 1181. *Dieppe 31km/19mi.*

Vannes   M7

Morbihan (pop. 44,000) Vannes remains much as it has been since the Middle Ages. The houses rise in tiers forming an amphitheatre above ramparts and moats, now turned into gardens, floodlit at night. The gabled houses are lavishly decorated with human and animal figures; the best are in the Place Henri IV, the rue des Halles and the rue Noé. The museum has a vast collection of prehistoric relics dug up in the district. The Promenade de la Garenne leads to the almost landlocked sea of the **Gulf of Morbihan**, 18,000 hectares/70sq mi of tidal water with more than 300 islands, some large enough to accommodate villages with hotels; others having nothing but a prehistoric cromlech or stone circle. Many steamer tours are provided in the summer. *Paris 460km/286mi, Rennes 105/68.*

NORTHERN FRANCE

The ancient provinces of Picardy, Artois and Flanders are, in comparison with the rest of France, of only minor appeal as regards natural scenery, though a closer investigation will reveal quiet beauty in the rich farmlands of the plains and the numerous, unspoiled woodlands. The man-made attractions are quite another story. This area is the cradle of the French nation, the scene of defeat and victory in 2000 years of struggle, culminating in the desolation of 1914–18. There is hardly a town or village which does not mark some tragic – or as often glorious – event in French history.

The coastline, low except for the chalk cliffs facing the Straits of Dover, has many pleasant resorts, notably Berck, Le Touquet and Wimereux, all unostentatious and less expensive than the famous places in Brittany and the south. Northern France was the birthplace of 19th-century manufacturing, but inland, away from the industrial and mining areas, are the ancient mercantile towns which should not be missed.

Flanders poppies

Fish or rabbit with prunes The fishing ports of the northern coast handle about half the fish eaten in France. Understandably, the best of the fresh catches gets into local restaurants, where it is served simply and without the sauces which some visitors regard with suspicion.

Market gardens flourish throughout Northern France, and the vegetables are superb. A great variety of soups in which vegetables predominate is served in every restaurant and café both at midday and in the evening; modest bars may offer soup and large chunks of fresh bread as the only hot food immediately available.

Unusual dishes are rabbit, cooked with prunes or cherries, in Flanders, and venison in the notable restaurants of the ancient towns of Picardy.

Festivals and Events March (first week), carnival of violets – Malo-les-Bains. April (last week), amateur film festival – Le Touquet; jazz festival – Dunkerque. May (first week), carnival – Amiens. May (last week), beer festival – Armentières. June 27, pilgrimage and processions – Boulogne. July (last week), fish festival – Boulogne.

Abbeville   H2

Somme (pop. 26,000) Abbeville straddles the Somme at one of the principal junctions of the roads of northern France. Carefully rebuilt after war damage, Abbeville is a delightful example of a Picardy town. It has many historical connections with England. In the cathedral of St Vulfran, Mary of England, sister of Henry VIII, was married in 1514 to Louis XII, to stabilize peace betwwen the two countries. In the First World War the Hôtel de Ville was the scene of major conferences between the Allied political and military leaders. Abbeville is a good centre for visiting the quiet little resorts on the bay of the Somme, *eg* **Le Crotoy** and **Cayeux-sur-Mer**, all within 30km/19mi. These villages were once important ports in the trade with England, Le Crotoy exporting boatloads of wood to the Cinque Ports. Some 10km/6mi north of Abbeville is the forest of **Crécy**, scene of the great English victory of 1346. The ford over the Somme, the camp of Edward III and the Black Prince, and the battle area are 1km/½mi north of the village on D111. *Boulogne 80km/50mi, Calais 124/77.*

Amiens   J4

Somme (pop. 136,000) The historic capital of Picardy is all too often just a name to tourists hurrying from the coastal ports to Paris and the South, whether they travel

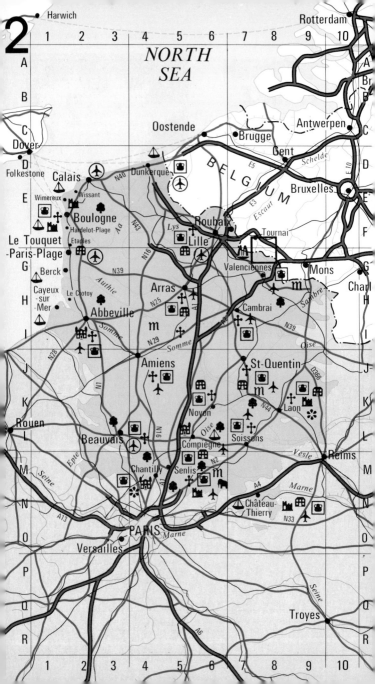

by road or rail. It is a beautiful and fascinating town despite its appalling sufferings in two world wars. In the 1914–18 war some 700 buildings were destroyed and in 1939–45 more than 4000. Dominating the town is the Cathédrale de Notre Dame d'Amiens, described by Ruskin as 'pure Gothic; exemplary, unsurpassable and uncriticable'. The main part was completed in 1270, and many additions were subsequently made. The 114m/375ft steeple was added in the 16th century. Nearby, in the Saint-Leu district, are Les Hortillonages, market stalls built over or alongside the numerous canals which intersect there. The gourmet is well catered for in Amiens, centre of a great farming area, especially with dishes based on duck, and with soufflés embellished with liqueurs.

Amiens is a good centre for visiting the First World War battlefields and war cemeteries. Within 40km/24mi to the east along route D929 are the towns and villages immortalized by the battles of the Somme – **Albert** with its Madonna and Child which miraculously survived on the summit of the church tower; **Thiepval**, with a memorial to some 73,000 British soldiers; and in contrast the tiny cemetery at **Mametz**, a half circle of graves of military bandsmen who were killed by shellfire as they stood playing for the columns moving to the front. *Boulogne 125km/79mi, Paris 155/96.*

Arras   H5

P-de-Calais (pop. 50,000) Arras stands in an area of France which has no particular beauty. It is a plain with a few hills and criss-crossed by streams and canals, with considerable industrialization. But the towns are old and beautiful, not least because they are the tidiest and cleanest in France. Arras, badly damaged like most other communities in this area in two world wars, has repaired with love and skill those buildings which did not escape destruction, so that the atmosphere of the 17th-century town which was ruled by Spain survives. The magnificent Grande Place reminds one of the older parts of Brussels, with its gabled and galleried merchants' houses and the beautiful Hôtel de Ville. At the side of the cathedral is a museum with examples of Arras tapestries and porcelain. *Calais 112km/70mi, Lille 50/31.*

Beauvais   L3

Oise (pop. 57,000) This is an impressive little town, a mixture of old and the new replacing air-raid damage in 1940. But the rather shabby old streets are embellished by the majesty of the cathedral of St Pierre, the highest in Europe and miraculously left almost unharmed by war. It is built on the ashes of a very early church destroyed by fire, the 13th-century builders determining to create a cathedral so large and strong that it would be indestructible. The roof is 43m/141ft from ground level – a project which would intimidate even modern builders. It did in fact require extra supports involving generations of work. The steeple toppled in the 17th century, and to this extent the building remains incomplete to this day. There are interesting tapestries and stained glass, and a remarkable astronomical clock. *Boulogne 166km/102mi, Dieppe 104/64.*

Château de Chantilly

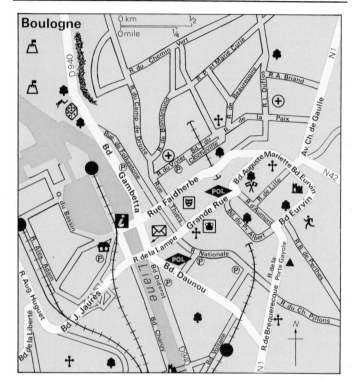

Boulogne E2

P-de-Calais (pop. 49,000) Boulogne is the
largest fishing port in France and is really
two towns in one. Basse Ville, along the
water, is a very modern and busy town
built on the ruins caused by 487 air raids
during the war. Haute Ville, on a steep
hill, rising behind the multistorey apartment blocks and business houses, was not
seriously damaged. The great walls, with a
pathway on the top, provide a good tour of
the old city. There are numerous hotels,
restaurants and cafés around the port area,
catering for travellers in transit. They are
often full during the season, and it can be
cheaper to drive along the coast, either to
Wimereux (the embarkation area for
Napoleon's proposed invasion of
England), 6km/4mi north, or **Hardelot-
Plage**, 10km/6mi south. *Paris 242km/
151 mi.*

Calais D2

P-de-Calais (pop. 80,000) From the 14th
century, when English troops captured
the town and it became an English posses-

sion for more than two centuries, Calais
has been almost as familiar to British
travellers as Dover. Few towns in France
have suffered so badly from enemy action,
and in both world wars it was devastated.
In the war years after 1940 the old town
and the harbour installations were completely destroyed. To the west of Calais is
the quiet little resort of **Wissant**, with a
fine sandy beach and large, inexpensive
hotels. *Paris 290km/180mi.*

Chantilly M4

Oise (pop. 12,000) On the D916 between
Amiens and Paris, Chantilly is famous for
the château built in the middle of a small
lake. This was the home of the Constable
of France, Montmorency, the real power
behind the throne of France during six
reigns. Another famous tenant was the
Duc de Condé, who came here for hunting. His stables for 240 horses and kennels
for 400 hunting dogs stand alongside the
château (open Mar.–Oct. daily except
Tues. and during race meetings). Inside is
the Condé Museum, containing a price-

ess 15th-century manuscript illustrating the seasons of the year – the *Très Riches Heures* of the Duc de Berry – a collection of miniatures by Fouquet, and one of the largest diamonds in the world – a pink-tinted jewel known as the *Grand Condé*. In the park, laid out by Louis XIV's landscape experts, is a 'toy village' of the kind Marie Antoinette had at Versailles. Beyond is the famous Chantilly racecourse. *Paris 43km/27mi.*

Château-Thierry N7

Aisne (pop. 14,000) This is the home town of La Fontaine, the writer of fables. His 16th-century house in the street named after him has been turned into a museum. The town is a place visited by many Americans. In the First World War US troops had their baptism of fire and held the line at Hill 204 and Bellau wood, adjacent to the town. *Paris 92km/57mi, Reims 62/38.*

Compiègne L5

Oise (pop. 41,000) Compiègne is deeply involved with France's history. From the days of Charlemagne it has had political and military importance. Joan of Arc was put in a cell here before her execution. Napoleon chose it as the place to marry Marie Louise before he took his bride to his capital. The Empress Eugénie made it the political and social centre of France. Louis XII built the Hôtel de Ville (note the figures which move out to mark the passing of each quarter hour on the 17th-century clock). Inside are two unusual museums, one displaying tens of thousands of lead soldiers from Roman

legionaries to French paratroopers; the other antique vases. In the château, built by Louis XV as his third most important palace, is the best collection of First Empire furnishings in the country. In one wing is a museum of horse-drawn and motor vehicles.

Compiègne has a magnificent beech and oak forest. On a spur of railway track running into the trees is the **Clairière de l'Armistice** where Germany surrendered in 1918, and France in 1940. *Paris 75km/47mi.*

Dunkerque D4

Nord (pop. 84,000) Dunkerque (Dunkirk), the third port of France, is famous as the last stand of the British forces in 1940 against the German armies. Its present site was below the sea until the 7th century when natural coastal change and reclamation created an area for a fishing town, and later a privateer base. It was almost completely destroyed in 1944 and has been rebuilt as one of France's most carefully planned industrial and residential towns. *Calais 40km/25mi, Paris 290/180.*

Laon K8

Aisne (pop. 30,000) Built on a massive hill, Laon was a free town and the capital of the last kings of the Carolingian dynasty (until AD 987). The massive 13th-century ramparts remain, with the moat laid out with walks and gardens. The streets and alleys in the old town are steep and winding, sometimes becoming stairways. Scores of beautiful houses of the 15th to 18th centuries are in a state of perfect preservation, and there are numerous old churches,

Laon Cathedral

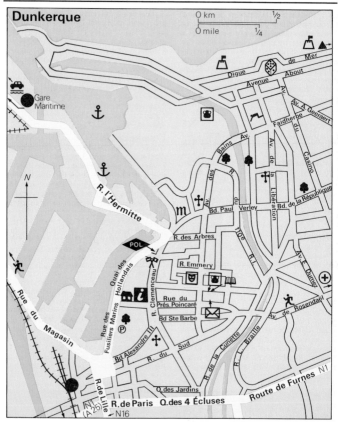

convents and abbeys requiring days for appreciation. The 12th-century cathedral is the best example of Romano-Gothic architecture in the country. Facing it is a very modern building – an arts and leisure centre. *Amiens 115km/71mi, Reims 77/48.*

Lille   F6
Nord (pop. 177,000) Lille is primarily a great industrial town, but the old district, built in the Flemish style when Spain ruled the area, is largely unspoiled by industry or war. The Bourse, between the Place Général de Gaulle and Place du Théâtre, is a magnificently ornate 17th-century building. In the church of St Catherine is the famous Rubens painting *The Martyrdom of St Catherine.* The museum vies even with the Palais du Louvre in its treasures. Rubens, Goya,

Van Dyck are among the artists whose paintings may be viewed there. *Paris 220km/136mi.*

Noyon   K6
Oise (pop. 14,000) Noyon has survived attacks in two world wars and innumerable skirmishes for centuries before. The cathedral is early 13th-century and stands in a square where the bishop's palace, the religious library, the cloisters and priests' houses still remain as they must have been in all medieval cathedral cities. Noyon was the birthplace of John Calvin, whose house is now a museum. *Amiens 63km/39mi, Laon 54/33, Paris 90/56.*

St-Quentin   J7
Aisne (pop. 69,000) This is an old town named after the 4th-century martyr buried in the basilica. Despite its position

on the Somme, some of the town's buildings managed to survive the shellfire of the First World War. The Hôtel de Ville is 15th-century, and adjacent to it is the Collégiale Church, lovingly perfected between 1230 and 1450, with wonderful stained glass windows. The Entomology Museum has a superb collection of butterflies. *Amiens 73km/45mi, Paris 140/87.*

Senlis   M5
Oise (pop. 15,000) A mere 51km/31mi from the centre of Paris, Senlis has the appearance of a remote provincial town, thanks to the beech woods which conceal it. The Romans had a big settlement here, possibly before they had managed to capture Paris. The remains of the arena indicate that accommodation for at least 10,000 spectators was provided. After Charlemagne became ruler of France he relaxed in the palace he built here, and it remained the principal royal seat within a day's riding distance of Paris until Versailles was built. In the grounds of the largely ruined château is a museum devoted to hunting. *Lille 172km/107mi.*

Soissons   L7
Aisne (pop. 32,000) Soissons is a magnet for war veterans and their relatives. The town was badly damaged in both world wars. The tower of the cathedral was destroyed and the nave partially reduced to rubble. The building has however been restored to its 13th-century perfection. In the choir is Rubens' *Adoration of the Shepherds*. In the rue de la Bannière is the memorial to British dead in the battles of the Marne and Aisne. *Paris 100km/62mi, Reims 57/35.*

Le Touquet-Paris-Plage G2
P-de-Calais (pop. 30,000 in summer) Adjacent to the fishing town of **Étaples**, this is a resort which was once the monopoly of the wealthy but now caters for everyone. It has two casinos, a racecourse, several night clubs and one of the largest swimming pools in France. Surrounded by dunes and pine woods, the town's promenade stretches for very nearly 2km/1mi; beyond it are magnificent sands spacious enough for land yachting and riding. The sandy coast extends from the airport for 14km/9mi, passing smaller resorts – **Merlimont, Stella Plage** and **Berck** – offering a quieter and cheaper holiday. *Boulogne 28km/17mi.*

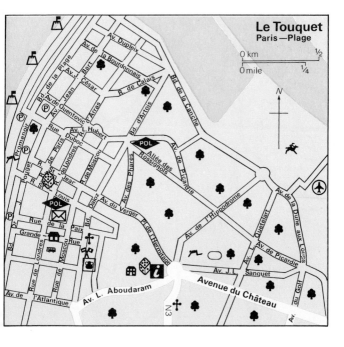

Le Touquet
Paris—Plage

THE ÎLE-DE-FRANCE

Despite the steady expansion of Paris since the war, control over urban sprawl has kept the surrounding region commendably unspoiled. The new departments into which the area has been divided are in no sense of the word suburbs but have retained their historic character.

Largest of the departments is Seine-et-Marne to the east of the capital. Rural in appearance, spread around the two rivers, it includes the forest of Fontainebleau. This district has long been a favourite of artists, largely because of the diversity of its terrain and natural features. On the south is Val-de-Marne, still peaceful along the Seine and Marne with numerous woods. On its west border Essonne is criss-crossed by rivers and streams along which lie some pretty villages. Tucked away between Essonne and the Paris area proper is Hauts-de-Seine, with modern industry and apartment blocks. On the west is Yvelines covered in forests and farmlands. Versailles and a dozen magnificent châteaux from France's era of the Sun King are within this department.

North of the capital are two small departments: Val-d'Oise and Seine-Saint-Denis. The former is heavily forested and scarcely affected yet by urbanization, its handsome old towns bordering the Seine and Oise. Seine-Saint-Denis was once one of the most fertile farming areas of the country. Urbanization has largely taken over, but all around St-Denis, centre of history and religion, the country remains much as it has been for centuries.

Eating and drinking locally The international approach to cooking found in Paris restaurants applies also in the Île-de-France. Opportunities for generous but basically simple meals are outstanding – this because Parisians, on a day out, like to finish the day with a generous repast. Bistros are numerous, and in the villages most hotels have good restaurants open to non-residents. But don't expect a hasty meal at these: the French like to spend at least an hour over luncheon and twice that time for dinner.

Festivals and Events Horse racing. There are eight racecourses in the region: Auteuil (hurdles): mid-February – end of April, end of May – mid-July, mid-October – mid-December; Chantilly: June; Enghien (hurdles and trotting):

February – December; Evry: March and October; Longchamp: Sundays April – October (no racing some Sundays in July and August); Maisons-Lafitte: July and mid-September; St-Cloud: April – October; Vincennes: mid-week in mid-February, mid-August, mid-September, mid-November.

May (last week to first week of June), music, opera, and drama festival – Versailles. May and June, classical music festival – St-Denis. June, concerts, ballet, variety and art presentations – Provins. June (mid-month), festival of roses – L'Hay les Roses. July (first Sunday), illuminations and night festival – Versailles. July (each Saturday), costume plays at night beside river – Moiret-sur-Loing. August (first two weeks), drama festival – Fontainebleau. November 3, St-Hubert hunting festivals – Chantilly, Compiègne, Rambouillet.

A perfect setting for horse racing

Dampierre   I4

Yvelines (pop. 750) A short distance off the N10 from Paris to Chartres, Dampierre lies in a valley of orchards and vineyards. The imposing medieval château (rebuilt in the 17th century) is the ancestral home of the Ducs de Luynes. As is the case with so many mansions refurbished in France's era of regal glory, the formal gardens were laid out by the Versailles expert, Le Nôtre. *Versailles 20km/12mi.*

Fontainebleau   K6

Seine-et-Marne (pop. 20,000) The palace ranks with Versailles and the Palais du Louvre as France's largest monuments to the era of kings. The building was started by Francis I in the 15th century, and a host of Italian experts were brought to France for the work. Famous historical figures are connected with Fontainebleau. Catherine de Médicis, Marie Antoinette and Josephine lived here. Napoleon bade farewell to his officers and bodyguard in the courtyard when he went off to exile.

As this was a royal hunting lodge it is surrounded by the game forest, a vast area of unspoiled woodland, containing rock formations large enough to attract mountaineers, a few tiny hamlets and serene glades. Every road, riding track and foot path is carefully marked, and despite the thousands of people who enjoy this area, it remains unspoiled. The *Route Ronde* is a signposted car tour. *Paris 65km/41mi.*

Melun   J6

Seine-et-Marne (pop. 40,000) Built originally on an island in the Seine, the town was once English, captured by Henry V in 1420 and held for ten years. The medieval city was built on the right bank and has many lovely buildings, including a church dating from the early 11th century. The modern town on the left bank suffered heavy damage in 1944. Standing on the edge of the forest of Fontainebleau, Melun is an excellent centre for combining walking and riding with visits to Paris. *Paris 55km/34mi.*

Pontoise   H4

Val-d'Oise (pop. 30,000) Standing alongside the Oise on one of the principal routes into Paris, this is a popular evening resort

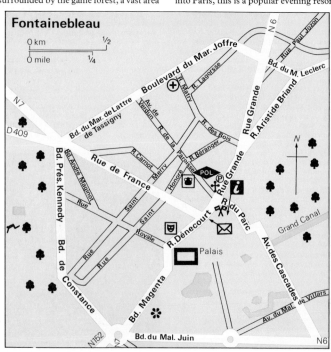

Gilded Door Entrance, Fontainebleau

for Parisians, despite surrounding industrial developments. Its churches are worth inspection. St Maclou is a flamboyant example of 14th-century style, though much of the building is 12th-century. Notre Dame has the well known statue of Notre Dame de Pontoise and the 12th-century tomb of St Gautier. *Paris 30km/19mi, Rouen 90/56.*

Provins   J8

Seine-et-Marne (pop. 13,000) Provins is the French 'city of roses'. There are numerous nurseries in the vicinity which present a remarkable sight in mid-summer. Most English roses have Provins stock somewhere in their ancestry, and the most famous rose of all is the red rose of Lancaster, introduced to England (and embodied in the coat-of-arms) by a 13th-century Duke of Lancaster who by marriage was also Count of Provins. The city is built on the site of a Roman township, though the strongpoint called Le Tour de César is actually 12th-century. *Troyes 73km/45mi.*

Rambouillet   J3

Yvelines (pop. 20,000) Rambouillet is on the N10, 51km/32mi south-west of Paris. The tourist often speeds past the little town on the autoroute but it is well worth a visit. The 14th-century château was once the rural retreat for Henri II and

Catherine de Médicis. Marie Antoinette loved the place. For Napoleon it was the last home he had in France before going into exile on St Helena. The château is the summer residence of the President or for distinguished foreign guests as a respite from Paris. If no one is in residence the rooms are open to visitors. The park is always open from dawn to sunset. *Orléans 90km/56mi.*

St-Germain-en-Laye   H4

Yvelines (pop. 40,000) St-Germain-en-Laye, 22km/14mi west of Paris on the N13, has the best view of the capital that there is from the terrace running through the town's park, designed by Le Nôtre, the man responsible for the gardens of Versailles. The château contains a beautiful little chapel built by St Louis and the room where Louis XIV was baptized. The young Mary Queen of Scots and the exiled James II lived here. The building is now the state's Museum of National Antiquities. 8km/5mi nearer Paris is the **Château Malmaison**, Josephine's favourite residence, with magnificent gardens originally laid out and stocked in the English style. The house contains art treasures and many relics of Napoleon and his consort, displayed just as they were when Napoleon lived there. Open daily, except Tues.

Versailles   I4

Yvelines (pop. 97,000) Although modern industries and ramifications of government have created a busy, thriving town sprawling almost as far as ¹Paris, the Versailles which the tourist sees is not so much a city as an enormous complex of buildings devoted to the institution of monarchy. Built by Louis XIV, Le Roi Soleil, its development necessitated changing many square miles of land – hill levelling, lake excavating, draining and tree-planting. Work began in 1661 and took 21 years to complete: the most perfect combination of buildings, gardens, statues, lakes and fountains, and carefully contrived natural scenery ever achieved by man. Versailles was France itself: every minister, general and government official had his existence 24 hours a day in the palace. Inevitably Napoleon occupied the palace to symbolize his power, and as inevitably the victorious Kaiser William I deliberately had himself proclaimed Emperor of Germany in the Hall of Mirrors in 1871. Nearly 50 years later Germany signed formal surrender after World War I in the presence of President Wilson, Lloyd George and Georges Clemenceau. Today, meticulously restored, Versailles is both a wonderful museum and a memento of a type of glory which has gone forever. It is also a superb example of the artistry of man when money, time and talent are available in unrestricted abundance. If time is short, the visitor is advised to visit the gardens and **Le Petit Trianon**, a palace in miniature, with its 'toy village' alongside. A tour of the palace takes at least four hours, but whatever is omitted the Royal Chapel, King's Private Apartments, and the Hall of Mirrors are an essential experience for every visitor to France. Open daily except Mon. 0945–1700. *Paris 22km/14mi.*

Galerie Française, Fontainebleau

THE LOIRE VALLEY

The Loire, the longest river in France, flows north in a wide curve from its source in the Cevennes until it bends west at Orléans. The valleys and gorges through which it flows thus extend for more than 1020km/630mi, draining one-fifth of France. However, the 'Loire Valley' of tourism traditionally refers to the section from Orléans to Nantes, and has been called the 'Garden of France'.

In summer the river flows gently between sandy banks and little islands, though in winter and early spring it can be capricious and can cause considerable flooding. This seasonal watering of the surrounding land creates a countryside of great beauty and fertility.

The Loire Valley is, of course, a great centre of secular and religious architecture. The cathedrals of Orléans, Chartres, Tours and Bourges are accepted as amongst the finest religious buildings in the country, while the luxurious châteaux of French kings and their ministers typify an era of peace and security when the castles of earlier times evolved into gracious palaces. This is a gentle region, where man and nature have co-operated to create a unity of beauty.

Not the least attraction to the tourist with limited time at his disposal is that the château country – 'the soul of France' – occupies a comparatively small area. Travel from one attraction to another takes little time, while within a few minutes' drive there will be a quiet village along the river bank with good accommodation and food.

Veal escalope and Muscadet The restaurants are numerous and good, and the area is popular both with overseas tourists and Parisians out for the day. A quite unusual feature is that in the riverside villages there are gardens attached to cafés and restaurants where *le five o'clock* is offered during the afternoon – tea and beautifully made pastries.

There are also plenty of modest cafés serving quick meals – savoury *crêpes* and a great variety of sausages, both hot and cold. The veal escalope, so often the choice of non-French speaking visitors in any restaurant from the Channel to the Mediterranean, is really good in the Loire valley, as indicated by the many French people who order it. Some gourmets even claim that coq au vin is better here than

anywhere else. The cheeses are good, especially those made from goats' milk; Sancerre and St Maure are outstanding.

The Loire Valley produces excellent wines. On a warm day Muscadet can be a good choice.

Festivals and Events *Son et Lumière* presentations at the principal châteaux take place at Easter and some weekends up to mid-June, thereafter usually nightly until mid-September.

Late April, 24-hour motor cycle race – Le Mans. May 7–8, Joan of Arc Festival – Orléans. May, students' pilgrimages – Chartres. May–June, international music and drama festival – Bourges. June (first week), international choir singing festival – Tours. June (mid-month), 24-hour motor race – Le Mans. June (last week), ballet and drama festival – Laval. July–August, drama and dance festival – Amboise. August (mid-month), horse riding – Châteaudun. September–October (Saturdays), classical music – Chartres. November (first week), wine fair – Nantes.

The Loire, Amboise

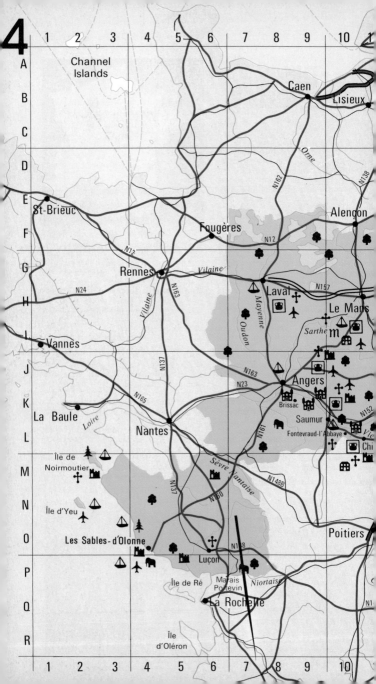

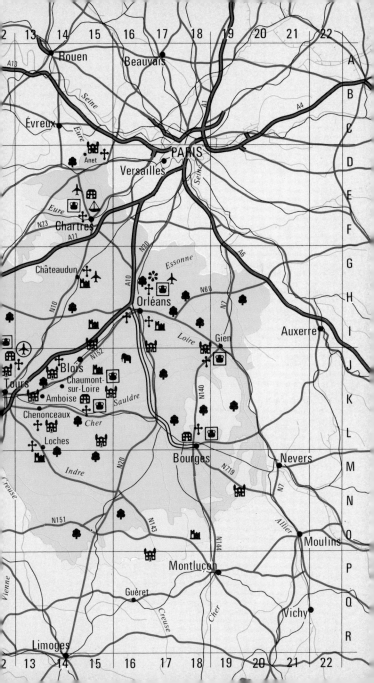

Amboise K13

Indre-et-Loire (pop. 11,000) Birthplace of Charles VIII, Amboise has one of the most important châteaux of the Loire Valley. Charles added Italian ornamentation so that the building is the first in flamboyant Gothic style. Later both Louis XII and Francis I added new wings. The chapel contains the presumed bones of Leonardo da Vinci, who spent the last years of his life in the château of Clos-Luce, now a Leonardo museum (in rue Victor Hugo). *Blois 34km/21mi, Tours 24/15.*

Anet D15

Eure-et-Loir (pop. 2000) 16km/10mi north of Dreux, this château which Henry II began in 1548, was one of the wonders of France. It was a gift to his life-long mistress, Diane de Poitiers. The double monogram of H and D can be seen in many places, and over the gateway is a copy of Cellini's portrayal of Diana the Huntress (the original has been removed to the Palais du Louvre). Originally the château stood on three sides of an immense courtyard, but two wings were destroyed in the Revolution as hated symbols of royal extravagance, although the pavilion, vinery, and chapel remain. Most of the decorative fabric is in white and black marble, emblems of mourning, as Diane was a widow. Her tomb is in the chapel; her body was disinterred by the revolutionaries and the remains scattered outside the château. *Paris 85km/53mi.*

Angers J8

Maine-et-Loire (pop. 143,000) Angers, the capital of Anjou, is the meeting place of the principal roads of the châteaux country and therefore an excellent centre in which to stay. Dominating the town is the enormous fortress/château on a hill overlooking the confluence of three rivers – Loir, Sarthe, and Mayenne – which in turn join the Loire on the south side of the town. More than 1000 years ago the Angers château sheltered the forebears of Angevin and Plantagenet kings, whose perpetual wars left the building in partial ruin. In the 13th century it was rebuilt, with the addition of the massive double walls and 17 watchtowers which stand today. In the castle precincts the royal courtyard has been turned into a museum of tapestries. The 77 pieces of Nicolas Bataille's tapestry of the Apocalypse are among the supreme masterpieces of this medieval art. The art gallery at 12 rue de Musée is in a building where the townsfolk lodged their distinguished visitors: among them Cesare Borgia, Mary Queen of Scots, and Catherine de Médicis. The paintings include the works of David d'Angers. Ceramics and glass are among the exhibits in the archaeologica museum (Place Rochefoucauld), and the building itself is of great interest. It is the oldest hospital in France, a masterpiece of 12th-century Angevin architecture. *Le Mans 90km/56mi, Nantes 90/56.*

Blois J14

Loir-et-Cher (pop. 52,000) Blois rises in a series of terraces above the river, sandwiched between a cathedral and a château The religious buildings are of particular interest because they range from the 10th-century crypt of the cathedral to the 20th-century basilica. The château presents differing styles over several centuries The Great Hall is part of the original home of the Counts of Blois; the States General met here in the late 16th century The battlements and chapel were built at the instigation of Louis XII, who was born in Blois. The staircase and the wing to which it leads are regarded as the exemplary work of French architecture in the first decades of the 16th century. Most of the rooms which remain intact are used to display arts and crafts, including many paintings of the Renaissance and sculptures which were in parts of the château since ruined or rebuilt. *Paris 180km, 112mi, Tours 58/36.*

Bourges L18

Cher (pop. 80,000) Bourges will inevitably be visited by every tourist of the Loire Valley if only because all roads seem to pass through it. Even 2000 years ago it was a large and wealthy community which resisted the Roman invaders far longer than other Gallic towns. Captured, it was named *Avaricum* by Rome and fortified as a military centre. When Charles VII was driven out of Paris, Bourges became his military headquarters until Joan of Arc brought him victory over the English.

The town is a maze of narrow streets and alleys with medieval buildings at every turn, the houses of the wealthy merchants and aristocrats frequently having picturesque courtyards, spacious gardens, and pretty fountains. The most imposing is the Hôtel Jacques Coeur built by one of Charles VII's ministers (1440–50). It is the finest example of a 15th-century mansion-cum-mercantile establishment in France. Part of the building is a museum, and several other medieval buildings serve in the same way the 15th-century merchant's house, Hôtel Lallemant (furniture and tapestries) Hôtel Cujas, originally built for a 16th-century Florentine merchant and later the residence of Jacques Cujas, a professor at the university. Dominating everything is the cathedral of St Etienne, which view with Chartres for Gothic perfection. Five doors (the centre surmounted by the famous *Last Judgment* sculpture) lead to five naves of equal and immense height. The stained glass is regarded as a complete example of the craft between the 13th and 17th centuries.

Brissac K8

Maine-et-Loire (pop. 1700) South of the Loire on the D748, Brissac is a small village clustered in the valley of the River Aubance around the magnificent castle of the Cosse-Brissac family, who still own it today. The most distinguished member of the family was Charles de Cosse-Brissac, Marshal of France in the early 17th century. He rebuilt his family home, emulating the royal residences of Henri IV and Louis XIII in size and luxury. The tapestries and furnishings are notable.

Chartres F15

Eure-et-Loir (pop. 41,000) This is the town with the loveliest Gothic cathedral

in Europe. Notre Dame was built with the money provided by untold thousands of pilgrims and completed in the 13th century. The hundreds of statues both outside and inside deserve hours of study, and the stained glass as long. It would be a pity, however, not to have time also to view the many medieval houses, the 12th-century food and wine cellars (of Loëns), and the city gates. The vast 17th-century bishop's palace close to the cathedral is a museum with sculptures, religious relics, paintings and tapestries.

45km/28mi south, on the N10, is **Châteaudun**, an enormous château guarding the northern approaches to the Loire Valley. A fortified castle existed here from the earliest years of the Christian era. The present size is due mostly to the work of Dunois, the companion and supporter of Joan of Arc. His descendants, the Dukes of Longueville, added to the accommodation and furnished the interior with 16th-century

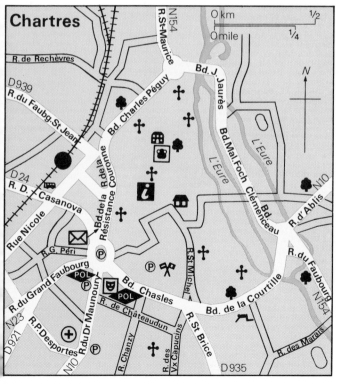

craftsmanship. Later the château fell into decay. Twenty years of painstaking work by the government have restored it to its original state. *Orléans 72km/45mi, Paris 90/56.*

Chaumont-sur-Loire   K14

Loir-et-Cher (pop. 800) From the river banks the château of Chaumont looks ominous and terrifying, as no doubt its 15th-century builders intended. Inside it is a fine and spacious residence with glorious views over the countryside it dominates. The visitor can appreciate why it was never assaulted as he walks up the narrow road clinging to the side of the hill and approaches the massive towers, battlements and outer bailey, finally passing over a drawbridge. The château has been lived in for five centuries without a break. It was the scene of silent hostility between Catherine de Médicis and her husband's mistress, Diane de Poitiers (see ANET AND CHENONCEAUX). *Blois 18km/11mi, Tours 41/25.*

Chenonceaux   K13

Indre-et-Loire Chenonceaux is not only one of the loveliest, but the most romantic, of all the châteaux of the Loire. When Normandy was an independent dukedom Thomas Bohier, the finance minister, saw a small castle on this site beside the River Cher and determined to have it. Cunningly he achieved the ruin of the owners, the Marques family, and little by little gained possession of all the land. He then pulled down the buildings, with the exception of the keep and the water mill, and erected his château. King Francis I seized it in 1535, and his son Henry II gave it to his mistress, Diane de Poitiers. She spent a fortune on extending the building, including an ornate bridge across the river. When her royal lover died, his wife, Catherine de Médicis, ousted Diane and elaborated the bridge with its present gallery. Until the Revolution, Chenonceaux was the scene of sumptuous royal feasts and celebrations exceeding in lavishness even those of Paris and Versailles. *Amboise 12km/7mi, Tours 30/19.*

Chinon   L11

Indre-et-Loire (pop. 8000) Chinon is a pretty little town on the banks of the River Vienne, where the houses are crammed together amid a maze of alleys and narrow streets. In the centre is the Grand Carroi from which one sees 15th-century buildings wherever one turns – a glimpse of a shopping and business area of five centuries ago. Walk down the streets leading to the river where there are the timbered homes of the wealthy inhabitants of those days. Both Joan of Arc and Rabelais, who knew Chinon well, seem very real in this town. The great attraction of Chinon is its grim, enormous château built on the crown of the hill. Once past the walls it will be seen that there are in fact several castles, each separate and each able to defend itself whatever happened to the others. Henry II of England died in the part called the Grand Logis, and local belief is that Richard Coeur de Lion was carried here after being mortally wounded when fighting in the Loire valley. The Coudray Château is in ruins, but a chimney and fireplace mark the room where Joan of Arc met her King, Charles VII, and inspired him to fight on. *Tours 45km/28mi.*

Fontevraud-l'Abbaye   L10

Maine-et-Loire (pop. 2000) This is of special interest to British visitors because of the monastery's close connection with England. Buried here are Henry II (the tomb sculpture is the oldest effigy of any English monarch), Richard Coeur de Lion and Isabelle, wife of King John. The building was both a monastery and convent. The huge church served both orders, but the best preserved buildings are in the monastic section. There are cloisters, cells and a kitchen. *Angers 70km/43mi, Poitiers 75/47.*

Gien   I19

Loiret (pop. 15,000) Gien was severely damaged during attacks in 1940 and 1944, and has been carefully restored with the modern buildings embodying the remains of those of the 15th century. Note, for instance, how the new church of St Pierre has been built around the massive 15th-century belfry. The château escaped damage. It was built to the orders of a woman, Anne of Beaujeu, in the 15th century and has an unusually feminine appearance. The fabric is a mixture of stone and multicoloured bricks built in a variety of patterns. Amusing little steeples and highly ornate doors add to the charm of the building. Inside is a small museum devoted to the history of hunting. *Auxerre 87km/54mi, Orléans 63/39.*

Laval   G8

Mayenne (pop. 54,000) Laval is an ancient fortified town with a 12th-century citadel and a church with notable 11th-century frescoes. The old town is on one bank of the river, and well separated from the burgeoning industrial complex on the other side. *Angers 73km/45mi, Rennes 70/43.*

Loches   L13

Indre-et-Loire (pop. 7000) The great treasure of the medieval town is the town (the part known as Haute Ville, which overhangs the newer buildings below) is

CHÂTEAUX OF THE LOIRE

Chenonceaux

Angers

Amboise

Loches

the triptych (1485) in the church of St Anthony, a work of art on which no price can be set. The town is full of almost comparable treasures discovered at every turn of a walk inside the walls. A glance at the position on the left bank of the Indre, with the junction of roads converging on the other side, indicates why this town was so heavily fortified to strengthen the natural defences. Only on the south side could attackers hope to gain a foothold. Here Gauls and Romans excavated ditches; in the 11th century the keep and ramparts were built; between the 13th and 15th centuries the massive towers and

forts. Behind them (still almost as perfec[t] as when they were built) a conglomeratio[n] of buildings grew up to form a château[.] They include a church, St Ours, whic[h] has a curious 12th-century roof consistin[g] of two hollow pyramids. The Oratory o[f] Anne of Brittany is particularly note[-]worthy with elaborately sculptured walls[.]
Tours 41km/25mi.

Le Mans   H1

Sarthe (pop. 155,000) Le Mans is famou[s] as the site of the annual 24-hour moto[r] race (there is an astonishing museum o[f] old cars – most in working order – adjoin[ing]

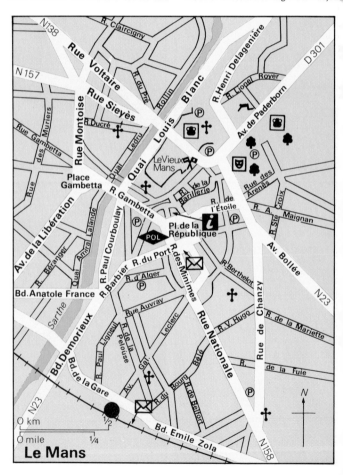

Le Mans

ng the track). But the town itself was famous long before the motor age. The old part is in reality a living museum and so full of interest that guides are available to take visitors around (information: Hôtel de Ville). Most of this section is enclosed by a Romano-Gallic wall, still intact. Notable houses are the Hôtel du Grabatoire (the canons' hospital), the Maison du Pelerin, the Adam and Eve House (1520), the Hôpital de Coeffort (built by Henry II of England) and the Hôtel de Vaux. The cathedral of St Julien is largely 12th-century; Berengaria, wife of Richard Coeur de Lion, is buried here. There are many tapestries. The former bishop's palace in the rue de Tessé is now a museum and includes some fine medieval silverware.

Orléans   H16

Loiret (pop. 110,000) Orléans was almost wholly destroyed in 1940 and has been rebuilt with great care to combine the spaciousness of modern planning with the style of its medieval glory. The town is a flourishing centre of the wine, agriculture and textile industries, but its fame rests on Joan of Arc, the peasant girl who inspired the successful defence of the city beseiged by the English. Her victory in 1429 is celebrated on or near May 8 with France's greatest annual fête. No trace of Joan remains beyond a statue in the spacious large city square, and in the Gothic style cathedral (rebuilt in the 19th century). Orléans is a good centre for visiting many châteaux and ancient churches. The oldest church in France (800 AD) is at **Germigny-des-Prés**,   48km/30mi south. There are châteaux at **Sully, Cléry, Talcy** and **Ménars**.

Saumur   K10

Maine-et-Loire (pop. 24,000) On the south bank of the Loire where the river divides to form an island, Saumur is a centre of the finest vineyards of the châteaux country. The town is rich in religious buildings, including Notre-Dame de Nantilly, with splendid tapestries, and the 12th-century church of St

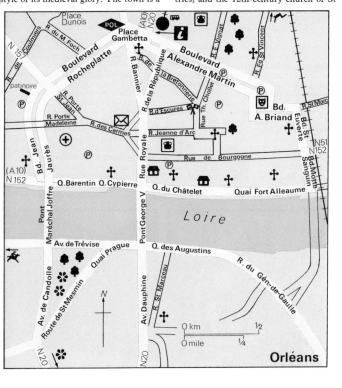

Orléans

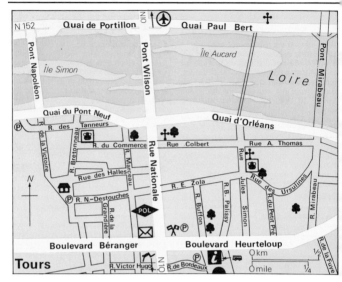

Pierre. In the château overlooking the town are two museums: one devoted to porcelain (including Limoges enamel of the 13th century), the other to horses and equitation. The building was constructed to the order of a 10th-century Count of Blois and Touraine. It was rebuilt four centuries later. Beside the river is a World War II tank museum (open daily). *Paris 300km/186mi, Tours 62/38.*

Tours   K12

Indre-et-Loire (pop. 145,000) This is the accepted centre for visiting the châteaux country. From the earliest times of the Christian era the town has been a centre of religious pilgrimage. It is the burial place of St Martin, a soldier of Constantine armies who became the first great monk of France. The old basilica dedicated to hir was destroyed during the Revolution. Th cathedral (begun in the 13th century) ha wonderful stained glass windows. Th adjacent archbishop's palace is now museum devoted principally to painting In the suburb of **La Riche** stands th château of Plessis-les-Tours, built b Louis XI in 1463. Only the central pa remains, including the room where Lou died in 1483. The château houses tw museums: one of silk, the town's famou industry, and the other devoted to relics the King and of St François de Pau *Bordeaux 330km/205mi, Orléans 116/7.*

Orléans Cathedral

Tapestry of the Apocalypse, Angers

NORTH EAST FRANCE AND THE WINE LANDS

Burgundy, Champagne, Alsace, Lorraine, Franche-Comté – the names of the provinces carrying the main roads from the north to the Mediterranean, and from Paris to the rest of Europe, are synonymous with wine. The temptation may be to speed on one's way except perhaps for brief stops in the famous towns which contributed so much to the history not only of France, but of western Europe. But to hurry would be to miss a delightful region of gentle hills, wooded hillsides and a great variety of scenery around the rivers and numerous lakes.

On the east side, the Vosges and Jura Mountains bring contrast, with vineyards and cultivated land giving way to mountainside forests and low scrub below the silhouette of rocky peaks.

Although to the north and east there is considerable industry, the usual spread of ugly development is missing, and the immediate reaction once away from the busy arteries of traffic is a sense of calm and timelessness.

For those wishing to visit vineyards and cellars, the Côte d'Or is in the centre of an area between the rivers Saône and Yonne; here six vine-growing areas have existed for centuries, and all offer opportunities to visit.

Quiche and Champagne Two famous regional dishes are Reims pigeon pie made from a recipe used at coronation banquets after the king had been annointed in the cathedral) and grape pickers' stew, a vast meal of bacon, pork and vegetables served with ham and sausages. For less hungry folk ham baked in pastry or simply spiced sausages will appeal. Or, to mark the fact that one is in the champagne country, one can order pike braised in champagne.

In Lorraine almost every café and restaurant serve the famous *quiche* as it really should be made, though each area of Alsace and Lorraine will claim its recipe is the traditional one. But all are savoury and never served as a sweet. The crust is lined with bacon, topped with beaten eggs and cream, and often some slices of cream cheese are added. It should be eaten very hot.

Brillat Savarin, the first and possibly greatest French writer on food, called this 'the most mouth watering region in Europe', so it is difficult to select examples from the huge variety of superb dishes. But look for cabbage hot pot, liver dumplings, onion and bacon tarts, and chicken with mushrooms. None is unduly expensive, and all will satisfy the most acute hunger.

With names such as these regions enjoy there can hardly be any need to recommend their wines, available in such bewildering variety of kind and price that one is wise to ask the waiter's advice. As something of a novelty try non-sparkling champagne, and on days when a really refreshing wine is required Riesling is inexpensive and always reliable. Liqueurs are worth sampling, possibly to choose a bottle to take home. Framboise, made from raspberries, is almost insidiously attractive. Two others popular with the local people are Ratafia (made from walnuts) and Quetsch (from plums).

Festivals and Events February (last days), carnival of masked figures – Châlon-sur-Saône. May 8–9, Joan of Arc festival – Reims. May (last week), wine fair – Mâcon. June (two days in first two weeks), wine fair – Beaune. June (mid-month), international music festival – Strasbourg. July 25, St Christopher's Day celebration (blessing of the motor cars) – La Tour du Meix. August (first week), Alsatian wines fair – Colmar. August (last two weeks), plum harvest festival – Nancy and Metz. September (first week), ripe grape festival – Arbois. September (first week), folklore festival – Dijon. October 6, festival for town's patron saint – Reims. October (first week), contemporary music festival – Metz. November (first week), exhibition of wine – Reims. November 28, wine festival – Chablis.

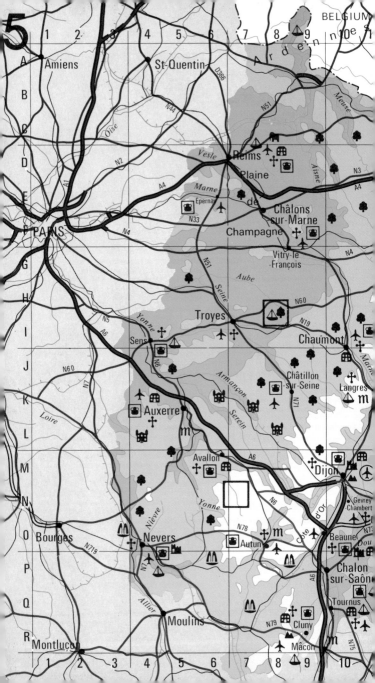

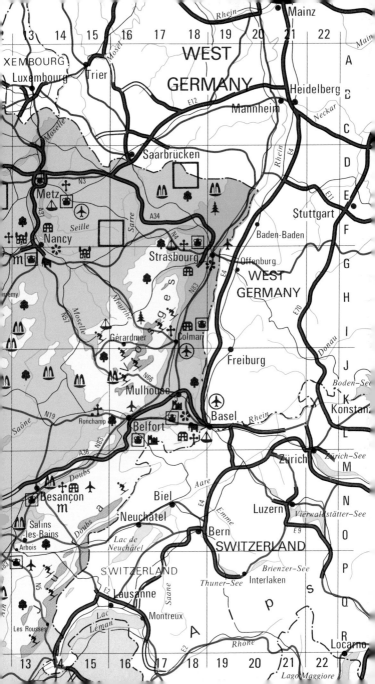

Autun   O8
Saône-et-Loire (pop. 18,000) Autun was once important enough for Julius Caesar to call it 'the sister of Rome'. Traces of the walls outside the present town indicate its great size before the Christian era. Some Roman buildings remain – the temple of Janus, two city gates and a small building resembling a pyramid, the purpose of which remains a mystery. The cathedral of St Lazare (12th-century) is famous for its sculpture of the Last Judgement over the doorway. *Dijon 90km/56mi.*

Auxerre   K5
Yonne (pop. 40,000) This medieval town is isolated by the A6 by-pass to safeguard its historic and environmental importance. The 13th-century cathedral is renowned for its stained glass and the fresco *Christ on Horseback*. The abbey church (12th-century) has the oldest murals in France; part of the building has been converted into a museum. A leisurely walk around the old town, lying along one bank of the River Yonne, brings glimpses of quaint streets and merchants' houses of the Renaissance period. 10km/6mi south at **Escolives** are new excavations of what was probably an important Romano-Gallic town; traces of a temple and baths have been revealed. *Dijon 149km/93mi, Paris 166/103.*

Beaune   O9
Côte d'Or (pop. 20,000) Beaune is the centre of the finest vineyards of France, whose wines are grouped under the name of Côte de Beaune. The town maintains the foremost wine museum in the world in the (restored) palace of the Dukes of Burgundy, the Hôtel des Ducs de Bourgogne. Apart from the exhibits, the building gives an impressive idea of the luxury of the life of this powerful family. Every year, in November, the Hospices de Beaune holds an auction of superb wines. They come from the vineyards owned by the charity hospital, housed in the Hôtel Dieu and founded in the 15th century. The rules, customs and costumes of the nursing sisters remain just as they were when the hospital began caring for the sick, but the vast wealth accrued from wine has provided it with the finest equipment and doctors in the country. The hospital has a museum of medicines and surgical instruments through the ages, as well as treasures donated by its founder, Chancellor of Burgundy, Rolin. The most important is Van der Weyden's *Last Judgement. Dijon 37km/23mi.*

Belfort   L16
Territoire-de-Belfort (pop. 57,000) Belfort has been a town beset by warfare since

Europeans had weapons. The fortifications built in the 17th century by Vauban are still impregnable. In the 1870 Franco-Prussian war the town resisted a siege of more than three months until peace was made. The huge bronze lion commemorating this event is the pride of the city; it was sculpted by Bartholdi, who cast New York's Statue of Liberty. *Base 70km/43mi, Besançon 90/56.*

Besançon   N13
Doubs (pop. 126,000) This was the perfect site for a town in less civilized ages. The River Doubs turns back on itself to make an almost complete loop. The only gap is protected by a huge rock rising to nearly 152m/500ft. On this rock the Romans built a fort, replaced in its turn by a medieval watch tower. At the foot of the rock stands the cathedral of St Jean (mainly 13th-century). Beyond its façade is a small Roman triumphal arch and then the Roman highway, now called the Grande Rue, stretching to the river bridge at the other end of the town. On each side are splendid examples of secular architecture of the Renaissance and the 17th and 18th centuries. Many of the houses have Spanish decorations and courtyards, a reminder that the town was once under the control of Spain. In the Place de la Revolution is an art gallery and archaeological museum. Besançon is a town of booming modern industries: watch making, aperitifs, plastics and dairy products. It is also a spa, with saline baths. Along the N83 and D72 is another spa **Salins-les-Bains**, and just beyond is **Arbois**, where Pasteur lived. His house is now a museum devoted to his early life and the discovery of anti-rabies vaccine. Another museum of Pasteur relics is in his birthplace at **Dôle**, 48km/30mi west of Besançon, on the N73. *Dijon 85km/53mi, Genève 156/97.*

Châlons-sur-Marne   E8
Marne (pop. 56,000) The town has a long tradition of wine-making, and is now the main town of the department. The cathedral is mainly 13th-century, with superb stained glass windows and priceless religious relics. The town's famous carillon of 56 bells, chiming age-old tunes over the town at regular intervals, is housed in the church of Notre Dame en Vaux. The Hôtel de Ville was the first resting place in 1921 of the Unknown Soldier of the USA. *Reims 43km/27mi.*

Châtillon-sur-Seine   K
Côte d'Or (pop. 7000) This has become a tourist centre since the discovery in 195 of the treasure of Vix, in a villag 7km/4½mi north west. The treasure now housed in the museum in the rue du

Bourg, comes from the tomb of a Celtic woman of high rank of the 6th century BC. The skeleton was lying in a chariot; her head-dress was of intricately worked gold. Alongside was a bronze urn, $1\frac{1}{2}$m/5ft high, with motifs and a frieze suggesting early Greek influences. This is one of the most important prehistoric art finds ever made in France. 60km/37mi north on the N19 at **Colombey-les-Deux-Eglises**, is Général de Gaulle's memorial and grave. *Dijon 82km/51mi, Paris 224/140.*

Cluny   R9
Saône-et-Loire (pop. 5000) Cluny now gives only a faint glimpse of the former glory of the abbey and its church. Once the abbey was the religious heart of Christian Europe, and the church was the largest Christian edifice until St Peter's was built in Rome. Only traces of the abbey remain, but the 12th-century church of St Marcel and the 13th-century Notre Dame are well worth visiting. *Lyon 97km/60mi.*

Colmar   I18
Haut-Rhin (pop. 68,000) A typical Alsatian town, Colmar combines all that is best in both German and French traditions. The hotels are clustered around the great cathedral, with its storks' nests perched on every vantage point of the roof and tower. Two minutes away is the carefully preserved medieval quarter full of painted and sculptured houses. The Maison Pfister, the shop and residence of some modest medieval butcher, is claimed with some justification to be the most beautiful house in the world. A little farther on is Alsace's 'Venice', an area where the houses are built above the waters of the River Lauch. The Unterlinden Museum, in a medieval convent, is full of priceless art, notably the works of the 15th-century painter Schongauer. Colmar was the centre of ruthless fighting in the closing weeks of the Second World War, but by a miracle little damage to historical monuments occurred. But a lovely old church in the town of **Ronchamp** (95km/59mi) on the N83 and N19 was destroyed. To replace it, Le Corbusier designed a remarkable modern chapel with the appearance of a ship in sail. *Strasbourg 70km/43mi.*

Dijon   M10
Côte d'Or (pop. 157,000) Dijon is the ancient capital of the Dukes of Burgundy, and now one of the great art cities of France. The ducal palace, the cathedral of St Bénigne, the churches of Notre Dame and St Michel, with the ancient houses surrounding them, give a glimpse of the old glories of this city. One of the many museums here is the Museum of Fine Arts, in the Salle des Gardes; it contains wonderful sculptures, paintings and art objects of the 14th and 15th centuries. Dijon today is also a centre of food processing. Cakes, blackcurrant liqueur (Cassis) and mustard are traditional specialities. *Lyon 190km/118mi.*

Langres   K11
Haute-Marne (pop. 12,000) Named *Andematunnum* by the Romans and *Lingons* by the Gauls, Langres stands on a steep promontory and is a fine example of a fortified town, with much of the ancient walls remaining. Diderot, the 18th-century philosopher, was born and educated here. The town has been famous for the manufacture of cutlery for seven centuries. *Dijon 65km/40mi.*

Mâcon   R9
Saône-et-Loire (pop. 40,000) This is the centre of the wine trade and, as a contrast, of French rowing. This 'French Henley' borders the River Saône which at this point flows placidly through a 275m/280yd wide channel and almost straight for $1\frac{1}{4}$km/$\frac{3}{4}$mi. North west of the town (8km/5mi) is the prehistoric valley of **Solutré**, which has given its name to a period of the Stone Age. Here, among the earthworks, are large rocky mounds. At the foot of the largest, the broken and sometimes charred bones of more than 100,000 wild horses have been excavated, relics of primitive man's ceremonial feasting here over centuries. *Lyon 70km/44mi.*

Metz   D13
Moselle (pop. 117,000) Metz, once Roman, then independent and finally a bastion of France, stands at the island-strewn junction of the Moselle and Seille rivers, and has many very ancient buildings. The church of St Pierre aux Nonnains (partly 4th-century) is the oldest basilica in France. The magnificent Gothic cathedral of St Etienne has two towers, from one of which a splendid view of the countryside is obtained – but it is 90m/295ft high and there is no lift. The A4 autoroute leads from Metz to the frontier. *Paris 330km/205mi, Reims 185/115.*

The expensive pottery of Nevers

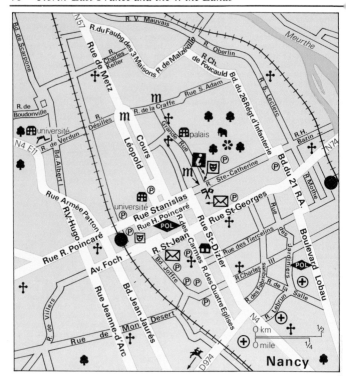

Nancy

Mulhouse   K18

Haut-Rhin (pop. 119,000) Mulhouse
flourishes today as an industrial centre. Its
prosperity started when it competed with
Lancashire in the production of textiles.
About 60 years ago the discovery of large
deposits of potash in the vicinity created a
vast chemical industry. A few traces of the
town's medieval ramparts remain, including the 14th-century Bollwerk Tower, a
guard fort on the walls. The most notable
attraction is the Hôtel de Ville, a painted
building with a covered staircase to the
main entrance and a very ornate 16th-
century council chamber. Two modern
features are a zoo set in a large park and
the dams of the hydro-electric plant on the
new Rhine-Rhône canal. The public are
admitted to the dams. *Dijon 215km/133mi,
Strasbourg 105/65.*

Nancy   F13

Meurthe-et-Moselle (pop. 112,000) This is
a spacious and beautiful town, thanks
largely to the devoted work of Stanislas,
the ex-King of Poland, who made it his

capital when his son-in-law, Louis XV
presented him with part of Lorraine fo
the duration of his life. Stanislas, in th
square named after him, created a vist
comparable with Versailles. Modern wa
has not seriously marred the beauty of thi
place, thanks partly to imaginative restor
ation. Places of interest include the Hôte
de Ville, the Lorraine Museum in th
Duke's Palace and the Cordeliers' Churc
where there are the beautiful tombs of th
Dukes of Lorraine.

This is the homeland of Joan of Arc
South west of the town is the village o
Domrémy, where she was born in 1412
A museum adjoins the tiny house in whic
she grew up. *Paris 312km/193mi, Reim
208/129.*

Nevers   O-

Nièvre (pop. 48,000) Nevers stands at th
junction of the Loire and Nièvre and ha
an Italian atmosphere, the reason bein
that the locality was in the possession o
the Italian Gonzaga family in the 16th an
17th centuries. The ducal palace is typ

cal. Under Italian inspiration France's first china factory was opened here in the 16th century, soon followed by glass works. The museum contains a unique collection of both crafts. The nearby convent of St Gildard is the burial place of Ste Bernadette of Lourdes. Her preserved body lies in a glass casket. *Paris 230km/143mi.*

Reims D7

Marne (pop. 184,000) For an earlier generation photographs of battered and smoking Reims, the damaged cathedral standing in timeless majesty above the ruins, symbolized France's resistance to the invaders of 1914–18. Historically, Reims cathedral transcends any other religious building in the Christian world. It took nearly 300 years to complete, and from the 13th century it was the most sacred building in France. All the country's kings were crowned there, and every invader, including the monarchs of England, knew that recognition before its altar would be the only way to confirm conquest. Reims invariably held out. The perfection of the cathedral, a mixture of austerity and a rich flood of statuary and sculpture, defies verbal description.

Reims is the centre of the champagne trade. Deep in the chalky earth on which the city stands are webs of long-established cellars, some extending for 16km/10mi and going 30m/98ft deep. There are even larger cellars at **Épernay**, 19km/12mi south. Visitors are encouraged to take conducted tours of these cellars where the champagne matures for the joy of man in his happiest moments. For information go to the Syndicat d'Initiative in Cour de la Gare, Reims or Place Thiers, Épernay. Ask also for the three famous champagne itineraries known as *Circuits Bleu, Rouge* and *Vert*.

A more modern place of interest is the Salle de la Reddition (10 rue President Roosevelt), the room in a school where Germany signed the surrender papers on May 7, 1945. *Châlons 45km/28mi, Paris 141/88.*

Sens I4

Yonne (pop. 27,000) Sens is the old religious centre of France. The cathedral is early Gothic (1130–60) and served as the model for Canterbury. The sculpture is lavish and the stained glass of a rare beauty. The cathedral's treasury includes the robes of Thomas à Becket, who took refuge at Sens, and of the archbishops of the diocese through the centuries. The shrouds of notable Christians from the 2nd century onwards are displayed in glass cases on the walls. *Paris 112km/69mi, Troyes 66/41.*

Reims Cathedral

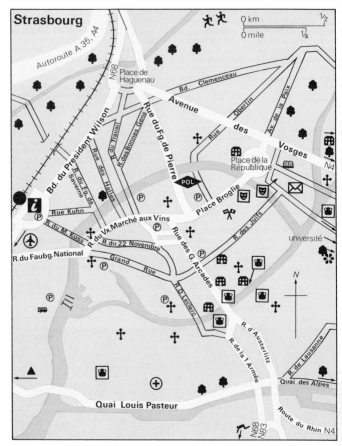

Strasbourg

Strasbourg   G19

Bas-Rhin (pop. 257,000) Strasbourg, one of the crossroad towns of Europe (though far from the sea it ranks as the fifth largest port in France), has many claims to fame. It is the parliamentary capital of Europe, a major centre of education, an industrial complex and an artistic centre. The Romans realized the strategic importance of this area on the left bank of the Rhine, and built a large city on the site (*Argentoratum*). Its prosperity came in the Middle Ages when it was a free city, using its enormous wealth to build churches, municipal buildings and luxurious residential houses. The supreme triumph was the cathedral, begun in 1277 and finished

in 1432. The 140m/460ft tower of pink sandstone is a Gothic masterpiece which should not be missed. A tourist attraction is the cathedral's astronomical clock with its parade of mechanical figures when noon is chimed. Many of the sculptures in the cathedral are copies: the originals have been placed for protection in the adjacent Muesum of Notre Dame, a group of medieval buildings with tiny courts, carved wooden galleries and quaint doorways. Among the treasures is a very old piece of stained glass showing a head of Christ.

Adjoining the museum is the Château des Rohan, an elegant and perfectly preserved 18th-century building. The luxury of the interior rivals that of Versailles, as it was intended to do. Part of the château is used as museums and an art gallery: the archaeological section covers the history of Alsace from prehistory; the gallery includes works by El Greco, Rubens, Rembrandt, Van Dyck and the Impressionists. In the decorative arts section is a remarkable collection of china, clocks and metal work. All around the cathedral the medieval town is carefully maintained as it was originally: covered footbridges over the tributaries of the River Ill, cool and darkened wine shops, ornately decorated inns and private houses. Some of the houses are open to the public; others are museums of Alsatian crafts, and of modern art.

Beyond this area is the Orangerie, a park designed for the Empress Josephine, who was not fortunate enough to see its beauty as today's tourists can under flood-lighting any summer evening. Bus and boat tours of the city, both by day and night, are arranged. Details of these and of any other item of interest from the information office, 10 Place Gutenberg.

Strasbourg is the ideal centre for visiting the wine country of Alsace. The wine road runs along the base of the Vosges to Colmar (93km/58mi); September and October are the busy months in the vineyards when 30,000 families, with helpers, gather the grapes. The Rhine road is shorter, with constantly changing views of the river. Huge constructional schemes were necessary along this route, for the completion of the final stages of the Grand Canal of Alsace. *Paris 460km/286mi.*

Tournus   Q10
Saône-et-Loire (pop. 7000) Tournus is a small, unspoiled medieval town with cobbled streets and innumerable old houses carefully marked by the authorities with the date and relevant details. The great attraction of the town is the remarkable L'An Mille Abbey, founded to mark the year 1000. It took two centuries to complete, and architects from as far away as Asia Minor contributed. Intended as a place of prayer and meditation, the interior is plain, vast and impressive. Enormous pillars of a dark pink stone support the arches of the lofty nave.

Troyes   I7
Aube (pop. 76,000) Troyes was the seat and capital of the Counts of Champagne, and one of the largest trading centres of medieval Europe. Henry V of England was married to Catherine of France in 1420 in the church of St Jean. This, and the cathedral of St Peter and St Paul, are remarkable examples of the Gothic style at its most flamboyant. *Amiens 275km/ 171mi, Paris 160/99.*

Vitry-le-François   G8
Marne (pop. 20,000) This is a unique example of medieval town planning. Francis I ordered it to be built, and employed an Italian architect to draw up the plans of every street, alley and house. The main objective was to create a defensive centre. Tragically the town was destroyed in 1940 and such reconstruction as had been possible was wiped away in 1944. The rebuilding has preserved the original street plan of King Francis. *Paris 180km/112mi, Reims 75/47.*

Champagne maturing, Épernay

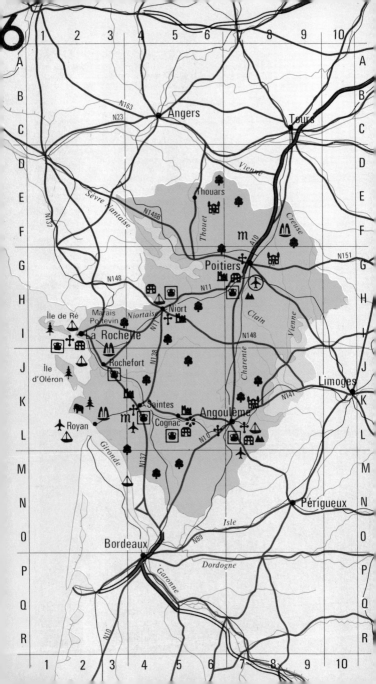

WESTERN FRANCE

Bounded by the mouth of the Loire to the north and the Gironde estuary to the south, the coastline of Western France bordering the Atlantic consists largely of fine sandy beaches, occasional stretches of rock, and islands and islets just off the mainland. The area extends for 600km/375mi. Inland the country is varied, with great vineyards, fields bounded by hedges reminiscent of farmlands in England, and several forests. For the visitor who prefers a seaside resort, the stretch known as the Côte de Beauté just north of the Gironde estuary is probably the best for initial exploration. The little resorts are sheltered by woodland stretching right round the peninsula. Further north and west of Niort is one of the strangest and most fascinating areas in France, Le Marais Poitevin (Poitou Marshes) – land reclaimed from the sea and criss-crossed by dykes – known as 'Green Venice'.

This area of the country is redolent with history. It has known battles with Roman legions and English archers. It was also a great religious centre and its churches and cathedrals are masterpieces of Norman architecture, notably in Angoulême, Luçon, Poitiers and Saintes.

Shellfish and Saintonge Fish and shellfish dishes are the specialities of this region, served in unique ways so that, familiar as the basic item may be, the dish is invariably unique. Oysters, for example, are fed on a special seaweed for years and are eaten with hot sausages, or cooked with garlic. Mussels are not simply simmered in a mild *bouillon* but dished in a thick cream sauce. Eels which swarm in the dykes and rivers of the Poitou Marshes are cooked with onions, garlic and egg white, in white wine. There is also caviar from fish caught off the Saintonge coast, and crab served with cheese.

A main course dish usually advertised simply as *farci* consists of boiled pork wrapped in cabbage leaves with spices, eggs, sorrel and lettuce among the items added to the stock to give flavour. For those who want simple food at its superb best – roast duck and green peas.

The wines of Anjou and Saumur are the local products to go with your meal. Try a bottle of Saintonge or Aunis.

Festivals and Events March (last two weeks), contemporary arts festival – Royan. May (mid-month), jazz festival – Angoulême. May (last week), open air drama festival – Niort. June (first week), yachting regatta and races – La Rochelle. July (first two weeks), music festival – Saintes. July, international arts festival – La Rochelle.

The Gironde

Angoulême   L7

Charente (pop. 51,000) Angoulême, the 'town built on a balcony', has immense ramparts devised to enhance the natural defences of this plateau rising above the valley of the Charente. The town is among the best examples of a fortified city of the Middle Ages. The 11th-century cathedral has been rather spoiled by 19th-century additions, but is basically a fine specimen of the Romanesque style. The museum beside the cathedral is an interesting building; it was originally the bishop's palace. Exhibits rather surprisingly include many items of folk crafts from Africa and Polynesia.

West of the town (5km/3mi) is one of the most remarkable churches in France, at **St-Michel-d'Entraigues**. Eight circular chapels stand on an octagonal base, with a cupola and lantern to cover them. The area was a centre of pilgrimage in the Middle Ages and this is the reason for the numerous chapels. *Bordeaux 108km/ 67mi, Paris 440/273.*

Angoulême Cathedral

Cognac   K5

Charente (pop. 22,000) A visit to the castle overlooking the River Charente gives some idea of the importance of a town which has given its name to brandy. The sheds and cellars where are stored the 20 million bottles produced each year stretch alongside the river banks. Visits are arranged but carefully controlled, for the cognac has to be kept in near darkness, in silence and at a constant temperature for years – sometimes several lustrums (periods of five years). The beautiful town park surrounds the ruined château of the Valois family, whose line became the monarchs of medieval France. Francis I was born here. 27km/17mi to the west is **Saintes**, already a flourishing Celtic town when the

Romans captured it. Roman baths, an amphitheatre and triumphal arch remain. The church is a masterpiece in the Romanesque style, with a crypt regarded as one of the finest in Europe. *Angoulême 42km/26mi, Bordeaux 113/70.*

Brandy ready for maturing, Cognac

Niort   H5

Deux-Sèvres (pop. 64,000) Niort stands on the edge of Marais Poitevin, an immense area of lush pastures criss-crossed by innumerable streams and canals (some of which were dug by the Dutch). Boatmen take tourists for a leisurely tour of about 1½ hours in flat-bottomed boats called *plattes*. They are stationed at various staging points (information: Place Poste). Niort is dominated by the remains of the immensely strong château-fortress built by Henry II of England; one of the towers is now a museum of local costume. The town is a famous centre for glovemaking and the curing of chamois leather. *La Rochelle 64km/40mi.*

Castle, Niort

Poitiers
G7

Vienne (pop. 85,000) Poitiers is in every English history book as the scene of the most vicious battle of the Middle Ages, when the Black Prince utterly defeated the King of France on September 19, 1356. The battlefield is 6km/4mi outside the town on high ground looking down on swampy land and vineyards. Poitiers was an essential capture for the English army of 4000 men fighting their way home from the wars; it was one of the biggest towns in western France, the capital of the Duchy of Aquitaine which stretched from the Loire to the Pyrenees.

Founded in the neolithic ages, there are dolmens and tumuli in the vicinity and pre-Christian pagan relics are mixed with early Christian memorials. In a Roman cemetery stands the monument called the *Hypogée des Dunes*, eastern in style and bearing a Romance language of the 7th century. Within the confines of the town there is the Baptistère St Jean, a place where converts were baptized from the 4th century onwards. In the church of St Hilaire is the tomb of the bishop of that name. He was the missionary responsible for bringing Christianity to Aquitaine. The interior of the church is a remarkable sight with seven naves and numerous pillars. Among the many other churches of the town is the magnificent Gothic cathedral, notable for its stained glass windows (12th-century).

The Palais de Justice is actually the old palace of the Dukes of Aquitaine. The wood-panelled hall must have been well known to the Black Prince, for it was built a century before him and refurbished during his life. Joan of Arc was accommodated in this palace and questioned on her divine voices in the adjoining house, the Maison du Maître Rabateau. As the result of the questioning she was put in charge of the army which marched on Orléans. Many houses in the vicinity of the palace and the cathedral remain much as they were when built during the Renaissance, and the four museums are crammed with unique items covering the 2000 years of the town's existence. There are so many sights tucked away in the narrow streets that instructions for a tour are essential. Information: 11 rue Victor Hugo. *Paris 336km/209mi, Tours 108/67.*

Notre Dame la Grande, Poitiers

La Rochelle   I2

Charente-Maritime (pop. 82,000) Known as the 'French Geneva' because of its citizens' strong Protestant profession of faith, this town is the fifth largest fishing port in France and, with the construction of the new Richelieu Harbour, rapidly becoming the major commercial port on the west coast, reviving its prosperity as a centre for trade with the USA and Canada.

La Rochelle has a proud and turbulent history. Originally the capital of the ancient province of Aunis, it became the property of the Plantagenets and thus came under English control. In the religious wars of the 15th and 16th centuries it was a Huguenot stronghold, resisting sieges which lasted for months on end, the most historic being that against the armies of Louis XIII, when Richelieu built a massive sea wall, still largely extant, to stop supplies reaching the beleaguered people by sea.

The old town is mainly of the Renaissance period, with covered pavements serving the commercial and civic buildings. In the old port the two 14th-century towers from which a massive chain was hung to prevent the enemy or pirates' vessels entering the harbour still remain. They are a contrast to the ruins of the submarine base built by the Germans in 1941–44.

Offshore are two islands. The **Île de Ré** (15 minutes by ferry) is a restful place of flowers, vines and pinewoods, with dunes and sandy beaches along the sea's edge. It was the scene of a major battle between the French and English in 1625, when the invaders were driven off leaving 2000 dead. The **Île d'Oléron**, reached by boat or more easily by a toll bridge some 40km/25mi south of the town, is the largest French island after Corsica. Warmed by the Gulf Stream, it is redolent with flowers, aromatic shrubs and thick woodland. There are eight good seaside resorts, all with splendid beaches. Offshore are the largest oyster beds in France.   *Angoulême   125km/78mi, Bordeaux 188/117.*

La Rochelle

SOUTH WEST FRANCE AND THE DORDOGNE

A glance at the map of France will indicate that the region south of Limoges and Bordeaux has few towns, and large areas are served only by minor roads. If man has not tamed and tailored this wild and beautiful country he has nevertheless established isolated settlements redolent of the turbulent history of wars great and small, of feudal warriors, and of people who have always regarded themselves as proudly individualistic.

This is a region all too frequently neglected by overseas visitors, though a favourite of French people who want a restful time or a bout of outdoor physical activity – both are there for the taking, and inexpensively.

First, the seashore. Between the Rivers Garonne and Adour, the Côte d'Argent is a sandy beach extending without a break for more than 225km/140mi, backed by sand dunes and the huge pine forests of the Landes. Then, on the short stretch to the Spanish border, the slopes of the Pyrenees meet the sea in broken cliffs and tumbling rocks pierced by creeks and inlets.

Inland, on hillsides and beside the many streams and rivers, are vineyards and orchards, pockets of cultivation amid untouched areas of forest and scrub, much of which is now protected.

In the heart of the area is the superb region where the River Dordogne tumbles through ravines or runs serenely and briefly through wooded valleys. Many of the trees bear chestnuts which are gathered in great quantities, and among the tree roots are the truffles for which the Dordogne is famed. The area is also a mecca for anthropologists, with the limestone caves and grottoes yielding some of the most remarkable discoveries of early man's existence.

Sparsely populated the south west may be, but the scattered towns and villages offer hospitality with a reputation unsurpassed in the whole country. Unrivalled towns are Lourdes, with its two million visitors a year and second only to Rome as a pilgrimage centre, and Pau, claiming with some justification to offer the finest landscape views in the world.

These two towns are on the edge of what many of the inhabitants would claim is ethnically a separate country – the land of the Basques, a mountain people. The growing popularity of walking, climbing and camping in summertime, and skiing in the winter, has brought tourism to many Basque villages.

Lampreys with leeks and Sauternes
The people of Bordeaux are fortunate in having every kind of food on the doorstep – fish and shellfish from the sea; meat, fruit, and vegetables from rich farmlands; and game from the country to the south and east. The best dishes of the town and surrounding tourist areas are fried whitebait, lampreys with leeks, roast lamb, entrecôte steak with a sauce, beef or lamb with parsley, chicken with artichokes, potatoes and onions, and duck's liver with grapes.

In the smaller towns inland and to the south game and poultry figure largely on the menus, with dishes based on beef as a speciality – notably steak garnished with beetroot, marrow and shallots, all cooked in red wine.

Closer to the Pyrenees pork and goose feature in dozens of dishes – a traditional one being *garbure*: a soup of cabbage, bacon, ham and pickled goose, served with chunks of coarse rye bread. Ham is prominently displayed in food shops: it is mostly eaten raw, as in the case of Bayonne ham, so one should be careful to specify that one wants cooked ham if that is a preference.

Tradition claims that mayonnaise was invented in this region, and the sauce is used on innumerable dishes – fish and poultry as well as salads.

One can hardly forget that the area is a producer of wines, for the vineyards are everywhere. Medoc, Graves and Sauternes are names familiar to everyone.

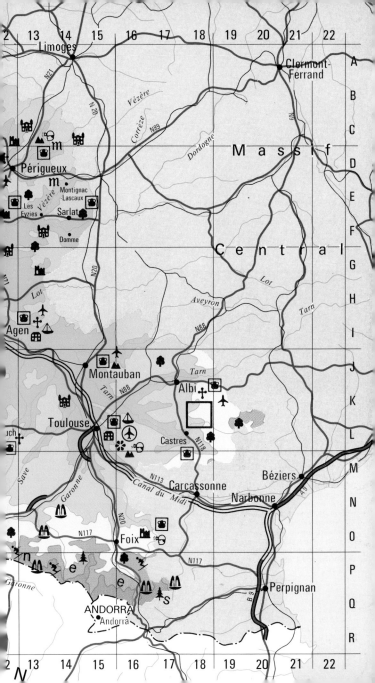

Festivals and Events March (last week), ham fair – Bayonne. Eastertide, gala – Biarritz. Eastertide, sacred music and arts festival – Lourdes. May (last two weeks), arts festival and trade fair – Bordeaux. June 20–27, Corpus Christi processions in many Basque villages. July (mid-month), dance festival – Brantôme. July (last two weeks), Basque folklore festival – Bayonne. August 15, festival of the sea – Arcachon. Biarritz. August 15, national pilgrimage – Lourdes. August (last two weeks), surf-riding championships – Biarritz. August (last week), sea festival – Biarritz. September (first week), music, dancing and drama festival – St-Jean-de-Luz. September 8, feast of the Birth of the Virgin – Lourdes. September (last weeks), wine festivals in all areas around Bordeaux where there are vineyards. December 24, Basque carols – St-Jean-de-Luz.

Beynac-et-Cazenac, on the Dordogne

Agen   I12

Lot-et-Garonne (pop. 36,000) The capital of the department, this is an ideal centre for exploring the Dordogne and the vineyards of the Bordeaux area, situated as it is on the junctions of the A62, N21 and N113. The town was established by the Romans as a military outpost. The winding, narrow streets have many medieval houses, four combined into a museum. The cathedral is 11th-century. Agen is famous for its preserved and crystallized fruits, especially prunes, and there are large orchards of plum trees all around. *Bordeaux 142km/88mi, Toulouse 108/67.*

Albi   J17

Tarn (pop. 50,000) Albi is a fortified town with a long history. Its most famous son is Toulouse-Lautrec, and the museum in the Palais de la Berbie contains the world's best collection of his works. The cathedral is a fine example of a fortified religious building, a vast edifice of brick. *Toulouse 76km/47mi.*

Auch   L12

Gers (pop. 25,000) The only town of any size in the wild and beautiful hinterland of south-west France, this is a welcome stopping place on the N21. The town clings to the sloping hills beside the banks of the River Gers, the streets often passing below buildings and through fortified gates – reminders of the time when the town was the capital of Gascony and the property of the kings of Navarre, always resisting France, to which the town was not united until 1598. Today it is renowned as one of the principal centres producing Armagnac, the 'bottled sunshine' brandy. *Bordeaux 181km/113mi, Toulouse 77/48.*

Biscarosse, the Landes

Bayonne   L4

Pyr-Atl (pop. 45,000) Bayonne is a busy little port at the junction of the Adour and the Nive rivers with massive ramparts (now set out as gardens and shaded by trees) encircling the ancient city. Within the walls are the fine Château Vieux, built on Roman foundations, and a 14th-century cathedral, reminiscent of Reims. The Bonnat Museum (rue Jacques Lafitte) has a wonderful collection of paintings and drawings by Rembrandt, Michelangelo, Botticelli and Dürer. Across the Nive is the Basque Museum. *Bordeaux 175km/109mi, Spanish frontier 32/20.*

Albi, Languedoc

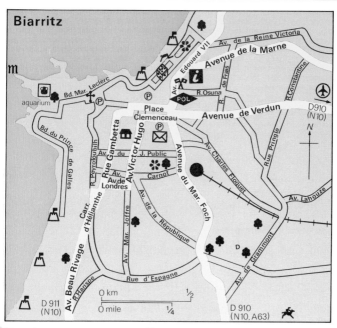

Biarritz L4

Pyr-Atl (pop. 27,000) Called 'the Queen of resorts and the resort of Kings', Biarritz became fashionable when Napoleon III went to live there. There is an old-fashioned elegance about the town with its beautifully-kept gardens and impressive hotels, but modern facilities are keeping pace. There are two magnificent swimming pools, one heated and open all the year. The four beaches of fine sand are sheltered by reefs which form a natural breakwater. The Marine Museum on a spectacular promontory contains a large aquarium. *Bayonne 8km/5mi, Bordeaux 183/114.*

River Leyre, the Landes

Bordeaux   F8

Gironde (pop. 617,000) Bordeaux is a busy port on the great curve of the Garonne as it flows to the Atlantic. The town has combined art and industry to make itself attractive to both the tourist and the businessman. In June it holds an international trade fair, following the international festival of music and dance in May. From May to July there is an international art exhibition. The town is of four eras: from Roman times there is a ruined amphitheatre (Palais Gallien); from the medieval period the Romanesque churches of St Seurin and St Croix and the Gothic style of the cathedral

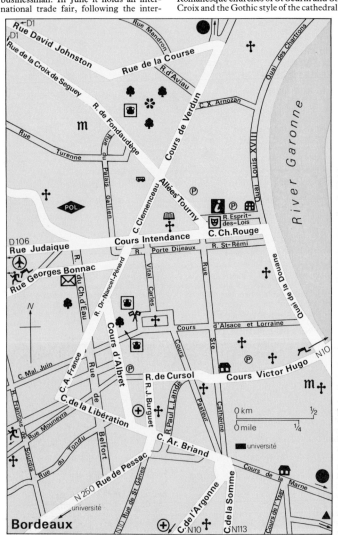

Bordeaux

of St André and the churches of St Michel and Ste Eulalie. In the 18th century the centre of the city was rebuilt in the classic style, exemplified in the Grand Théâtre on the Place de la Comédie. Post-war additions and reconstruction include a huge sports stadium, swimming pool and modern buildings replacing bomb damage. The Beaux Arts Museum in the Jardin de la Mairie has a fine collection of 18th-century paintings. *Paris 560km/350mi, Toulouse 250/155.*

Cauterets   O9
Hautes-Pyr (pop. 1000) Cauterets is a spa in the summer and a winter sports centre. The sulphur springs, used since the Roman era, were believed to cure sterility; now they are of benefit in bronchial and respiratory diseases. But it is more usual to see the fit and youthful in this resort, a centre for climbing. Ten climbs, ranging from the classification of 'easy' to 'guide essential', start from Cauterets.

Bordeaux

Foix   O16
Ariège (pop. 10,000) This is a community huddling around the old château of the Counts of Foix, which includes a museum of local relics, among them those from prehistory, giving an idea of the archaeological importance of this area. All around are enormous caves which have been inhabited from time immemorial. North on the N20 (turn left on D628 and D119) is the **Mas d'Azil**, an underground passage made by river water. It is 415m/1350ft long and rarely less than 30m/98ft wide. Man-made galleries branch out from the passage, the walls covered with prehistoric drawings of bison, deer, *etc*, and the floor a litter of the bones of mammoths and bears. The Calvinists hid here to escape persecution, and in 1940 the caves were used as an aircraft factory. Continuing along the D119, through St-Girons, are the **Gargas caves**. Man lived here about 20,000 years ago and performed horrible sacrificial rites, for on the walls are imprints of mutilated hands. *Toulouse 81km/50mi.*

Lourdes   O9
Hautes-Pyr (pop. 18,000) The town is situated between Pau and Tarbes in the foothills of the Pyrenees. Until just over a century ago Lourdes was a poverty-stricken, insignificant village. It is today one of the most important centres of pilgrimage in the world as the result of a vision seen on February 11, 1858, by a 14-year-old girl named Bernadette Soubirous. She was gathering firewood along the little river with a sister and a friend, when she heard a rushing wind. She turned and saw the figure of a lady surrounded by light in a grotto in the rocky hillside. Bernadette's own account of the vision was that she 'was a young and beautiful lady, clad in white, with a blue sash, her feet bare, but with a golden rose on each foot'. Altogether the child saw the vision 18 times. Instructions given to her included a direction to scratch away the earth over a rock. Here the famous spring has flowed ever since and a church was soon built over the spring. The church is large but of little architectural merit, and the decoration of the grotto is garish and crude. There is much commercial exploitation in the town, with its innumerable souvenir shops. But there is also a kindly and well run organization for the million pilgrims who visit the shrine every year; hotels are cheap and numerous; many are specially organized to deal with desperately sick and crippled people, and there are doctors, nurses and priests to ensure that every pilgrim is well cared for. Whatever his faith, the tourist cannot help but be impressed by Lourdes, especially at the peak pilgrimage time from August 15 to September 8. *Pau 40km/25mi.*

Basilica, Lourdes

Montauban   J15

Tarn-et-Garonne (pop. 50,000) Standing at the foot of the Bas-Quercy Hills, the town is one of the largest centres for the fruit trade in France. In the summer and autumn samples are given away to visitors free of charge. The local brick is a delicate pink colour and many of the old monuments are built with it, making them most attractive for colour photography. The bridge over the Tarn is 14th-century. The painter Jean Ingres was born in Montauban and the town has many relics of his life and a museum with his works. *Agen 72km/45mi, Cahors 60/37, Toulouse 50/31.*

Montauban

Montignac-Lascaux   E14

Dordogne (pop. 3000) This is the site of the decorated caves accidentally discovered by a boy and his dog in 1940. The prehistoric paintings cover the walls in a large cavern and in two narrow passages leading from it. These unique examples of art when bison and rhinoceros roamed south-west France deteriorated through the moisture from visitors' breath, and the caves are now closed to the public, but there is a full size replica of the cavern, and from July–Sept. films of the paintings are shown. To the west is the prehistoric site of **Les-Eyzies**, a narrow valley honeycombed with caves. The artists of Lascaux probably lived here, and many traces of habitation have been discovered. The relics are displayed in the 10th-century château (restored) which houses France's National Museum of Prehistory. *Limoges 100km/62mi.*

The Pyrenees

Pau   M8

Pyr-Atl (pop. 86,000) Pau stands on the
edge of a high plateau offering wonderful
views of the mountains. A fortress was
built in the 11th century to guard the ford
across the river below the town. Then a
large château was built on the site by the
Viscounts of Béarn. The boy who was to
become Henri IV was born here; because
of his unhappy childhood the place was
neglected after he ascended the throne.
Centuries later Louis Philippe spent large
sums on restoration. It is now a museum
with a rich collection of tapestries. *Lourdes
43km/27mi, Toulouse 195/121.*

The castle, Pau

Périgueux   D12

Dordogne (pop. 38,000) Périgueux was an
important Roman town, with an arena and
a temple to Vesunna, part of which survives. In the 4th century the town was
sacked by Vandals who took the stones of
the Roman buildings to construct a defensive wall. The cathedral of St Front has
oriental cupolas and pinnacles which were
added in the 19th century. The museum
in the Cours Tourny has a large collection
of prehistoric relics discovered in this
area, which has been inhabited since *homo
sapiens* existed. *Bordeaux 106km/66mi,
Limoges 102/63.*

St-Jean-de-Luz   M4

Pyr-Atl (pop. 12,000) On the border with
Spain, St-Jean-de-Luz has a vast beach
fringing a lovely bay, with a fishing harbour reaching deep into the heart of the
town. The boats bring in sardines and
tuna in quantity, and the local fish restaurants are understandably very good.
Louis XIV was married in the pretty
16th-century church. *Biarritz 15km/9mi.*

Tarbes   N10

Hautes-Pyr (pop. 58,000) A picturesque
stopping place for travellers on the N21 or
N117 and a convenient centre for a lengthy
visit to the spectacular scenery of the
Pyrenees. It is known as 'the town of the
horse'; its famous stud farm produced the
best strain of warhorses in Europe. The
scenery around the town is so spectacular
that viewing points for the panorama have
been developed. *Lourdes 19km/12mi, Pau
40/25.*

Toulouse   L1

Hautes-Gar (pop. 383,000) Toulouse is b
far the biggest and most important town o
the south west. There are many wel
preserved houses of the Renaissanc
period. The outstanding place of intere
is the basilica of St Sernin, as rich i
Christian relics as any place outside th
Vatican. The remains of 128 saints in
clude those of some of the Apostles. Th
most sacred relic is a thorn from the crow
of the Crucifixion. *Bordeaux 250km
155mi, Limoges 306/190.*

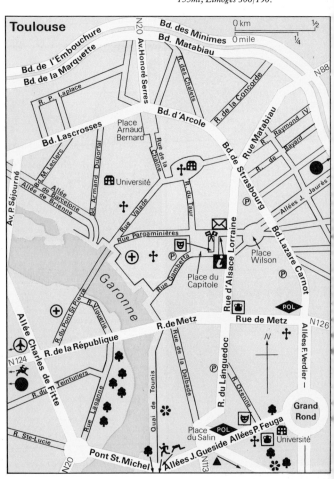

CENTRAL FRANCE

The heart of France rises from the fertile area of Périgord to desert-like terrain, and then to the mountainous region of extinct volcanoes – a geological phenomenon creating fantastic scenery of rocks, gorges, caves and waterfalls. Now only sparsely inhabited, this fascinating area was once quite densely settled thanks to the security from attack provided by the wild country-side. Early man lived in the caves; the Romans built military stations; and in the Middle Ages came the castles to protect communities. Religious architecture flourished in the 14th–16th centuries, the churches often combining traces and symbols of old pagan religions with those of Christianity. The conical hills, or puys, of lava and basalt, and the craters and gorges (many with mineral springs) make this neglected area a source of rewarding exploration both for the nature lover and the devotee of history. The Routes Nationales traversing the Massif Central give the merest glimpse of the grandeur of the scenery in its remoter areas. This is seen at its best in the National Cevennes Park and the Regional Volcanoes Nature Reserve.

Goose and Clafoutis The wildlife of the central provinces provides most of the traditional dishes – stuffed hare, trout served in a dozen different ways, partridge with cabbage, crayfish. The farms keep a lot of poultry, and chicken is featured on the average menu, sometimes in unusual guise such as chicken with crayfish. Goose is not just a Christmas food as in most of Europe. It is eaten all the year round – roasted with chestnuts, simmered in a vegetable stew, and made into gooseflesh and goose liver sausages.

Not many parts of France make much fuss about puddings. Limousin is an exception. *Clafoutis* is a pudding made from semolina and cherries but is, of course, available only when cherries are being gathered.

Festivals and Events March (last week), carnival – Vichy. May (mid-month), festival of Our Lady of the Haven ('Black Virgin') – Clermont-Ferrand. August 14 and 15, religious festival and pilgrimages – Le Puy. August 26, shepherds' festival – Lafont-Sainte.

Gorge of the Ardèche

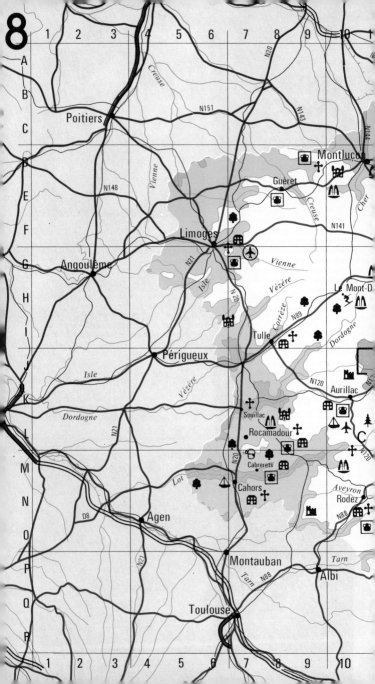

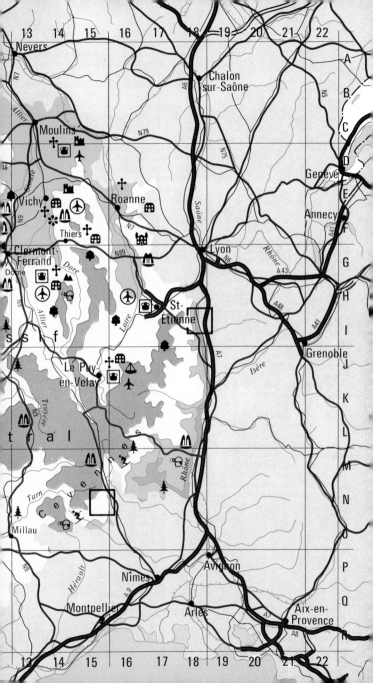

Aurillac   K10

Cantal (pop. 33,000) A typical town of the
Massif Central, Aurillac developed as a
resting place at important crossroads.
Tourists on the N120 or N122 will miss
much by failing to stop for a time in this
little town with its massive keep and
interesting 17th-century houses. It makes
an ideal base, as French tourists know but
foreigners have not yet appreciated, for
visiting some of the most spectacular and
unspoiled areas in the country. To the
north east are the Cantal Mountains and
the vast Regional Volcanoes Nature
Reserve. To the south (35km/22mi on
minor roads) is the largely deserted village
of **Conques**, once a major European
staging post for pilgrims, where stands
what is generally regarded as the loveliest
Romanesque abbey in France. *Clermont-
Ferrand 160km/100mi, Montauban 175/
109.*

Cahors   M7

Lot (pop. 22,000) Cahors, the Romano-
Gallic town *Divona*, is to many tourists
just a town on the road to the
Mediterranean coast and Spain, which is a
pity, because its buildings are both old
and remarkable – a 14th-century guard
tower, a fortified bridge and a magnificent
domed and cloistered 11th-century cathedral among them. Pope John XXII and
Leon Gambetta, hero of the defenders of
Paris in the 1870 war, were born here. To
the north west, in the **Pech-Merle** grotto,
are prehistoric paintings of horses and the
handprints of the artists. *Agen 91km/
56mi, Bordeaux 198/123, Toulouse 110/68.*

Clermont-Ferrand   G12

Puy-de-Dôme (pop. 161,000) Clermont-
Ferrand is a large industrial city processing rubber and chemicals. The Gothic
cathedral is 13th-century. 15km/9mi west
of the town is **Le Puy de Dôme**, a
volcanic mountain rising sheer for nearly
1500m/5000ft. Prehistoric man regarded
it as a sacred place, and there are traces of a
Druid temple on the top. After the Roman
conquest a statue of Mercury was erected
which was said to be as large as the
Colossus of Rhodes. The summit has an
observatory, restaurant, and viewing platform. *Lyon 180km/112mi.*

Limoges   F6

Haute-Vienne (pop. 147,000) For more
than eight centuries china has been made
here, with porcelain a later development
with the discovery of pure white clay at **St
Yrieix-la-Perche**, south of the town on
the D704. Limoges porcelain and enamel
work have gained a peerless reputation
and maintain it. There are daily visits to
the factories (information at 9 boulevard

Fleurus). The Musée Dubouché is devoted to china and porcelain, the municipal museum to enamel work. *Bordeaux
222km/138mi, Poitiers 118/73.*

Moulins   C13

Allier (pop. 27,000) The Counts of
Bourbon made this town their capital, and
it reached the zenith of its power and
wealth in the 15th century. The network
of ancient cobbled streets and houses
round the ruined château gives some idea
of Moulins' importance in those days. In
the cathedral are numerous ornate tombs
and superb stained glass commemorating
the Bourbon family, with the greatest
treasure the famous 15th-century triptych
by the 'Master of Moulins'. On the bell
tower (restored) the moving figures of
Jacquemart and his family mark the
hours, the half and quarter hours.
Clermont-Ferrand 95km/59mi.

Le Puy   J13

Haute-Loire (pop. 29,000) Le Puy is an
extraordinary sight as one approaches
across a plateau and sees the peaks of
volcanic lava rising straight upwards. On
top of one peak is a small chapel built in
the 11th century; on another a huge statue
of the Virgin, erected just over a century
ago. The cathedral of Notre Dame du
Puy, which appears to be clinging near the
pinnacle by supernatural means, is actually built into the side of the steep face of
the rock and constructed from blocks of
lava. The image of the Virgin inside the
cathedral is black and possibly a link with
some pagan goddess of the Middle East.
The whole building was the work of
Christian and Muslim architects – a
unique example of co-operation between
Christendom and Islam in a religious
building. Since the early Middle Ages, Le
Puy's Black Virgin has been the object of
pilgrimage. The procession up the long
flight of stone steps, with hooded penit-
ents, takes place every year on August 15.
*Clermont-Ferrand 130km/81mi, Grenoble
190/118, Lyon 135/84.*

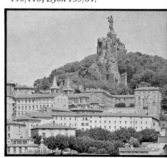

Le Puy

Roanne E16

Loire (pop. 56,000) Far up the Loire, this town grew as a port. Many of the medieval merchants' houses survive, but the château, built when this was the capital of a region, is partly a ruin. There is a considerable amount of modern industry in the suburbs which tends to conceal the inherent charm of the older part in the centre. 3km/2mi south of the town the Loire runs through spectacular gorges worth a visit. 19km/11mi north is the small town of **Charlieu** with a Benedictine abbey, regarded as one of the best examples of Cluniac style (12th-15th centuries). *Lyon 88km/55mi.*

Rodez N11

Aveyron (pop. 28,000) This capital of the old province of Rouergue stands on a hill overlooking a vast area of hills and plains. It was a twin city with the church owning one part and the local counts the other, massive walls separating them. The rivalry lasted until the reign of Henri IV. The cathedral, reminiscent of a fortress in its massive walls, is dominated by a magnificent bell tower (87m/288ft high) in flamboyant Gothic style. The interior of the cathedral has 14th- to 16th-century sculptures, some of which were sadly mutilated in civil wars. Within the ramparts, now topped by pleasant walks, are numerous ornate houses of the 15th and 16th centuries. *Aurillac 95km/59mi, Toulouse 55/96.*

Tulle I8

Corrèze (pop. 22,000) Tulle stands on the junction of several busy routes (N89, N20, N140) and is a good centre for visiting a large number of historic sites in the vicinity. The town itself is very old, with 15th-century houses perfectly preserved, the Gothic cathedral has been restored. To the east is spectacular country with extinct volcanoes and the grandeur of the River Dordogne at its wildest; all around are churches and religious buildings from the time this town was on a major pilgrim route. *Aurillac 85km/53mi, Limoges 90/56.*

Vichy E14

Allier (pop. 32,000) Vichy, briefly busy as the site of France's 1940–44 government, has reverted to its time-honoured role as a leisurely health resort. The nine springs of therapeutic and medicinal value were first extolled by the Romans, and have been popular ever since. The town's appeal to the wealthy sick resulted in Vichy being planned solely as a pleasure resort, with magnificent parks, theatres, concert halls and hotels. Today the thermal baths are state-owned, and the thousands of patients, old and young, are treated free. The *buvettes*, small salons built alongside the medicinal springs, provide water free to everybody who asks. Despite its being a centre for medical treatment, Vichy is not depressing in any way. The Vieux Parc, centre of the town, presents a gay, carefree appearance as visitors, and those wealthy enough to live here the year round, stroll among the flower beds and enjoy a cocktail before dinner and a night's gambling in the casino. The wide thoroughfare, Boulevard des Etats Unis, leads to the old town with many medieval buildings and the church of St Blaise which is partly new and partly very old. In the vicinity of Vichy are many areas of great natural beauty in the Dordogne valley. Some 32km/20mi north east on D907 is **Lapalisse**, with a large château. South of Vichy is **Thiers**, where almost every shop displays knives, forks and spoons, and visitors are welcomed in the small factories. In the rue de Barante is a knife museum. *Clermont-Ferrand 59km/37mi, Paris 340/211.*

Yoke of oxen, Thiers

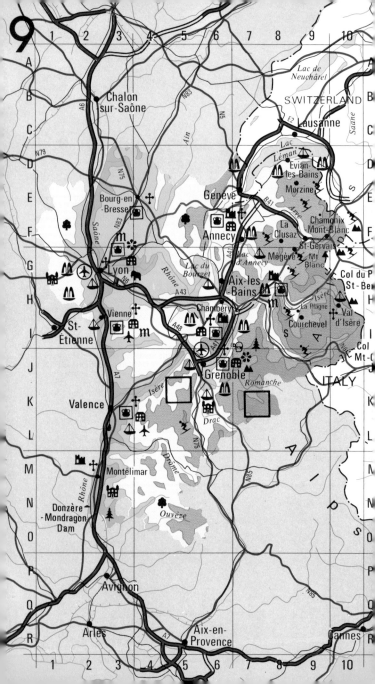

SAVOY AND THE RHÔNE VALLEY

The natural artery of the Rhône marks the western border of a part of France with great tourist appeal – to be appreciated immediately as one passes through its natural gateway at Lyon. Within sight are mountain peaks, some always snow-capped, rising to the majesty of distant Mont Blanc. In the land which lies before those ranges are forests, large lakes, deep gorges and stretches of pine woods interspersed with pastureland on which huge flocks of sheep feed during the summer. Many of the towns were founded by the Roman legions as military strongpoints, and many Alpine villages remain untouched by modern life. Even the barrages and canals, which have been constructed to tame and utilize the streams and rivers feeding the Rhône, have not greatly changed the age-old atmosphere.

The departments, including Savoie, the most popular for winter sports, form an enclave not typically French. It was 1860 before this region finally, after numerous wars, became part of France.

Tripe and Gamay The citizens of Lyon claim to be the most discriminating – and prodigal – gastronomes in France. The town has a host of restaurants awarded high distinctions, with prices to match. However, there are more modest establishments which also serve delicious food.

Perhaps the best-loved dish is Lyon tripe, cooked with onions grown around Roanne, rivalled only by chicken with truffles. There are a dozen famous dishes based on pork, *eg* a kind of sausage served with pistachio nuts and truffles, grilled chitterlings, the French version of black pudding, and hot ham with walnuts. Many of these dishes are available in neighbouring towns and villages as the Lyonnais like to drive out of the city into the countryside for a meal. Prices here are lower than in the fashionable places in the centre of Lyon.

To the east as one approaches Savoy food is simpler and often unique. Trout is available everywhere, and much of the meat is smoked, so can be bought for picnics. But the great foods of Savoy are the cheeses, especially Tome, Emmental and Beaufort (used as a fondue).

The entire Rhône valley produces a wide variety of wines. In Savoy there are wines one probably would not come across outside France. Charpignat and Ripaille (white) and Gamay (red) are worth ordering. As an aperitif or after-meal liqueur there are spirits made from cherries, plums or pears.

Festivals and Events Mid-February to mid-March, mountain music festival – Courchevel. March (mid-month), international Sarennes Derby (skiing) – Alpe d'Huez. March (last week), international trade fair – Lyon. Eastertide, music festival – Annecy. May (early), classical music festival – Évian. May (last week), spring fair – Grenoble. June (mid-month), traditional festival – Lyon. July, short films festival – Grenoble. July (third week), Alpine festival – St-Gervais-les-Bains. August (third week), carnival and flower festival – Aix-les-Bains. October (last week), autumn fair – Grenoble. December 8, Festival of the Immaculate Conception – Lyon.

The Aiguilles and Mer de Glace, Chamonix

Aix-les-Bains   G6

Savoie (pop. 22,500) A spa and health resort on the Lac du Bourget, Aix-les-Bains ensures that visitors have plenty to entertain them while they take the cure. There are cinemas, two casinos and a racecourse. The treatment mainly concerns rheumatic diseases. This is a resort catering for both the wealthy and those of more modest means. The Dr Faure museum has 19th- and 20th-century paintings. *Annecy 34km/21mi, Grenoble 46/29.*

Annecy   F7

Haute-Savoie (pop. 55,000) The ideal time to arrive in Annecy is shortly before dusk, when the town is bathed in half-light and the towering mountain ridge across the lake is rimmed with glowing pink. The town is a health spa and also a popular holiday centre with innumerable hotels of all categories, a delightful casino, and, of course, Lac d'Annecy. The old quarter, lying back from the lake, is a network of narrow streets full of chic shops. In most of these streets traffic is banned. The Syndicat d'Initiative, in the Place de l'Hôtel-de-Ville, provides details of the lake and the mountain excursions, but Annecy is definitely a place for leisurely walking – along the lakeside promenade or, more adventurously, into the unspoiled foothills of the mountains. *Genève 41km/26mi, Lyon 140/87.*

Old town, Annecy

Bourg-en-Bresse   E4

Ain (pop. 45,000) This mecca for French gourmets has more fine restaurants than any other place of comparable size. The speciality is sautéed frogs' legs. It is a charming old town and ideal for exploring both Burgundy and the Jura region. The church of **Brou** (now in a suburb of the modern town) is an extraordinary masterpiece by a Flemish builder; the lacy stonework, stained glass and carved woodwork are regarded as the finest examples of 16th-century religious art. *Lyon 62km/38mi, Paris 416/264.*

Chambéry   H

Savoie (pop. 57,000) This was originall the capital of the independent Duchy o Savoy. The castle, which was the seat o government, dominates the area. Th centre of the town is traversed by the ru de Boigne which has charming shoppin arcades on either side. The cathedral of S François-de-Sales (15th-century) has notable doorway. The adjacent bishop' palace is now a museum devoted to th history of Savoy. About 1km/½mi east o the town is the house where Roussea lived. It is maintained just as he and hi mistress, Madame de Warens, furnishe it. *Lyon 109km/68mi, Valence 125/78.*

Chamonix-Mont-Blanc   F

Haute-Savoie (pop. 9000) Chamonix jus tifiably claims to be the world capital o mountaineering and snow sports. Th first winter Olympic Games (1924) wer held here. Cable cars carry skiers to height above the town of almos 3400m/11,200ft, and only 600m/1970 below the summit of Mont Blanc, giving 28km/17mi run down again. Durin summer Chamonix is the base from whic to climb Mont Blanc, and for the les venturesome there are cable car rides ove glaciers to the border with Italy. Th Mont-Blanc tunnel is 7km/4mi south o the town. *Genève 86km/53mi.*

Évian-les-Bains   D

Haute-Savoie (pop. 6200) On the borde of Lac Léman (Lake of Geneva), Évian les-Bains is a comparatively small spa, bu offers plenty of amusement for visitor taking the cure. Its waters are used fo treating kidney diseases. The water i tasteless which is the reason why million of bottles of.it are sold every year throug out France as the normal refreshment t take with meals, either 'neat' or with win and soft drinks. *Genève 45km/28mi.*

Grenoble   J

Isère (pop. 400,000) Grenoble is a larg and spacious city on the Isère, which flow right through the town, and is surrounde by mountains which enable inhabitants t enjoy caving, climbing and skiing after short bus or car ride. Once the mai industry of Grenoble was glove manufac ture, but now it is a centre of scientifi research and of technological industrie Monuments include the 16th-centur Palais de Justice and the 12th-centur cathedral, with Stendhal's birthplac close by. The art museum has one of th most important collections of paintings i provincial France, including such mod erns as Gauguin, Matisse, Utrillo an Picasso. *Lyon 107km/66mi, Marseille 31 195.*

Lyon   G3

Rhône (pop. 1,300,000) The third largest city in France, Lyon avoids the ugliness of an industrial complex thanks to its two fast-running rivers, the Rhône and Saône, which join on the southern outskirts. The old town, with a history of 2000 years, stands on a steep hill of volcanic origin on the banks of the Saône. The hill is pierced by a modern road tunnel and the motorist from the north is unaware that he is in the centre of the city until he emerges on the river bridge. The old town has an imposing cathedral on the summit; behind it is an almost unspoiled area of 14th- and 15th-century houses. Between the two rivers is the heart of the modern city, mostly built in the 18th century and dominated by the Place Bellecour, one of the largest squares in the world. Under its tree-lined fringes, the Lyonnais stroll in the evening or listen to the band. Cafés and hotels surround the square, which has an information office in one corner of which one may book a bus tour of the town, ingeniously arranged to fill in a couple of hours before the night expresses and car sleepers leave for Paris and the Channel ports. Proud of its long history, Lyon devotes much care to housing and preserving its antiquities. Eleven museums display exhibits concerned with textiles, furniture, Roman relics, medicine, theatre, cars, printing, banking, natural history, armour, and painting. The Roman theatre is regularly used in June and July for concerts and classical drama. *Grenoble 109km/68mi, Marseille 315/195, Paris 465/288.*

Mégève   G8

Haute-Savoie (pop. 5000) Mégève is in a valley adjoining that in which Chamonix stands. The slopes are not so formidable as in the more famous skiing centre. With over 20 ski-lifts and cable cars, and the largest ski school in France, the area has increased in favour in recent years, and many luxury hotels have been built. *Annecy 60km/37mi, Chamonix 36/22.*

Montélimar   M2

Drôme (pop. 30,000) Montélimar, on the N7, is the world's nougat centre. Almost every shop sells the confection and anyone who strolls along the main street can enjoy free samples before the inevitable purchases. Nowadays the town has a new claim to fame. It stands between two modern dams and power plants, harnessing the forces of the Rhône. The most spectacular is the **Donzère-Mondragon Dam**, 5km/3mi south of the town, a complex of 20 dams and generating plants which have increased France's electricity supplies by nearly a third, and have transformed a large area of infertile land by

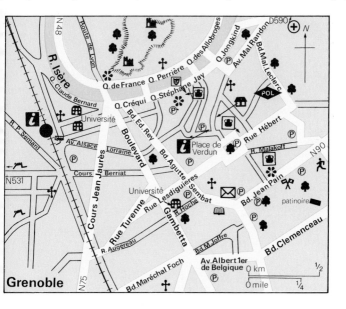

Grenoble

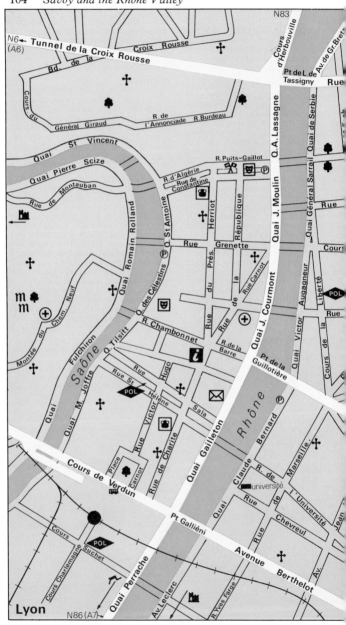

Lyon

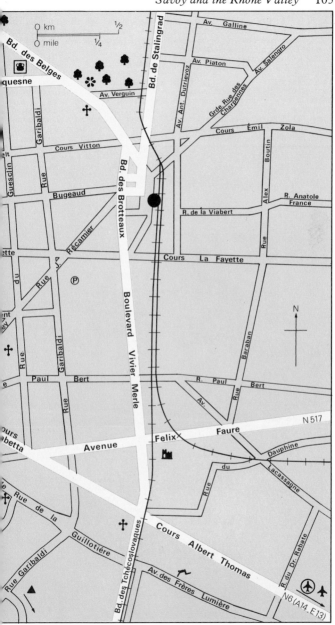

irrigation. Tourists can visit the dams on Saturday afternoons, Sundays and public holidays, but passes have to be obtained from the Compagnie Nationale du Rhône, 28 Boulevard Raspail, Paris. *Avignon 85km/53mi, Paris 608/377.*

Val d'Isère   H10
Savoie (pop. 1400) This tiny mountain village is now a popular resort, both summer and winter, for climbing and skiing. Within a radius of 10km/6mi are some 50 cable lifts serving the ski runs. Cable railways lead to peaks over 2400m/7900ft high. In summer the villag is the base for walking in the Vanoi National Park. *Chambéry 134km/83mi.*

Vienne   H
Isère (pop. 29,000) Vienne overlooks th Rhône and is of Roman origin. Th Temple of Augustus and Livia is perfect preserved; what was originally a hug theatre cleverly built into the slope of th hill on which the town stands is now a impressive ruin. The town has textile an glove making factories. *Lyon 28km/17m*

Mont Blanc

LANGUEDOC-ROUSSILLON

A sandy beach stretching from the Camargue to the Spanish border; 2750 hours of sunshine a year; 21 yacht harbours' – these well publicized assets have tended to focus attention on the coast. With 180km/110mi of virtually uninterrupted sandy beach, marked by quaint old fishing villages as well as carefully planned modern resorts, this is the area which draws tourists almost to the exclusion of other parts of Languedoc-Roussillon.

Inland, from the wild foothills of the eastern Pyrenees to the flatlands round the Rhône estuary, and north to the streams and rivers cascading through gorges and glens, dotted with many vineyards, there is a welcome contrast to holiday crowds and busy roads. Small communities and quite large towns alike have retained the old way of life. Within the two national parks, traditional villages and the natural environment are carefully preserved.

Most of France is steeped in history, but few regions more than Languedoc-Roussillon. Carcassonne is probably the best preserved medieval fortified town in Europe; Nîmes the best example of a Roman town outside Italy.

The new resorts include **La Grande Motte**, which has a lagoon for up to 1000 pleasure craft; **Cap d'Agde**, nestling beside an extinct volcano; **Gruissan**, built around an old village on a circular peninsula; **Leucate-Barcarès**, on a sea lagoon; **St-Cyprien-Plage**, developed around an old fishing port.

Partridge with walnuts and celery Anyone staying on the coast is unlikely to miss the memorable experience of a beach barbecue of sardines. Whatever one's opinion of the tinned version, a heap of these succulent little fish, crisped and piping hot, scooped up with bread and washed down with some of the superb wines of the district, makes a meal to remember.

The inhabitants are renowned for their prodigious appetites, earning their living with vigorous outdoor work. With reason it has been said that nothing which runs, flies or swims has been omitted from the menu, ingeniously cooked to produce a huge variety of dishes.

Sausages and pâtés are made from pork, liver, turkey, duck and goose – all excellent for a picnic lunch. Unusual dishes are often very localized and unlikely to be met with outside their tradi-

tional area – such as Carcassonne's braised beef with olives, the mutton of the Causses and the duck with turnips of Belcaire. Partridge, guinea fowl and quail are often served with walnuts and celery.

The wines of the region are varied and cheap, and some of the aperitifs are sold all over the world. The best-known cheese is Roquefort.

Festivals and Events Shrove Tuesday, processions and fair – Narbonne. March 20, battle of flowers and dance of the vines – Pézenas. Good Friday, processions – Céret, Collioure, Perpignan. May 23–25, gipsies' pilgrimage and festival – Les Stes-Maries-de-la-Mer. Whitsun, music festival – Béziers. Whit Monday, pilgrimages – Céret, Collioure. June 23–24, Midsummer night bonfires in most towns and villages. June 29, fishermen's and sea festival – Gruissan, Sète. July, drama festival – Carcassonne. August 15, festival and races – Les Stes-Maries-de-la-Mer. August (third week), wine festival – Banyuls-sur-Mer. September (last weekend), wine harvest festival – Nîmes. October (last two weeks), international wine fair – Montpellier.

La Grande Motte

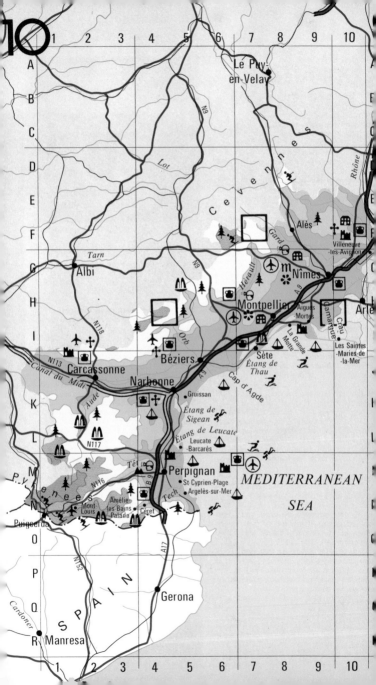

10

Le Puy-
en-Velay

Alès

Villeneuve-
lès-Avignon

Gard

Nîmes

Arle

Tarn

Albi

Hérault

Montpellier

Aigues-
Mortes

Crau

Camargue

N9

Lot

Cévennes

Rhône

N118

Orb

Béziers

La Grande
Motte

Les Saintes
-Maries-de
-la-Mer

Carcassonne

Canal du Midi

Aude

Narbonne

Sète

Étang de
Thau

Cap d'Agde

N113

Gruissan

Étang de
Sigean

N117

Étang de Leucate

Leucate
-Barcarès

P y r e n e e s

Têt

N116

Perpignan

B.9

St-Cyprien-Plage

Argelès-sur-Mer

MEDITERRANEAN

SEA

Mont-
Louis

Amélie-
les-Bains
Palada

Céret

Tech

Puigcerdà

N152

A17

S P A I N

Cardoner

Gerona

Manresa

Aigues-Mortes I9

Gard (pop. 4400) Aigues-Mortes lies among the salt marshes of the Camargue on the Rhône estuary. The town looms up on the horizon of the vast plain, an unspoiled medieval city with bastions and ramparts which have stood untouched for ten centuries. Crossing the moat the tourist enters through the huge fortified gate and moves along narrow, winding streets. Once Aigues-Mortes was a great port, but the sea has receded for some 5km/3mi. From Aigues-Mortes two famous crusades – of 1248 and 1270 – set out under the leadership of St Louis whose statue stands in the main square. Louis built the huge Tour de Constance, one of the most massive medieval fortresses still standing. It was used as a prison for Protestants in the 18th century. In one cell, cut into the 3m/10ft thick walls, the word *Resistez*! scratched by a prisoner still stands out white on the grey stone.

Beyond the salt flats (reached by car from Arles on the D570) is **Les Saintes-Maries-de-la-Mer**. Legend has it that the sisters of the Virgin and of Lazarus landed here in AD 40. With them came their Negro maid, Sarah, the patron saint of the gipsies. From May 23–25 Romany tribes collect here from all over Europe and immerse an effigy of Sarah in the sea. There is a museum of the Camargue, and a large zoo. *Nimes 40km/25mi.*

Amélie-les-Bains-Palalda N3

Pyr-Orientales (pop. 4000) This ancient village has recently developed into an important resort because of its superb views and exotic vegetation, with oranges and pomegranates growing among fields of mimosa and sub-tropical flowers. The River Tech flows through awe-inspiring gorges and lush valleys. The N9 and D115 run through this spectacular area leading to a number of memorable villages, notably **Céret**, where in 1910 Picasso, Braque and their friends lived, calling it the 'Barbizon of Cubism'. *Perpignan 37km/23mi.*

Argelès-sur-Mer N5

Pyr-Orientales (pop. 5000) This is a pleasant little town set back from the sea and a good base for exploring the wild area of gorges and valleys north of the Pyrenees. There is a small casino open in the summer. *Perpignan 21km/13mi, Spanish border 16/10.*

Carcassonne J2

Aude (pop. 46,000) The town lies, serene and ageless, in a vast hollow between the foothills of the Cevennes and Pyrenees – the historic wonder of France, with the centre surviving in, or lovingly restored to, its pristine glory as created between the 9th and 13th centuries. Its massive walls, forts, keeps and storehouses give a vivid idea of what life was like in the troublous Dark Ages, and it is easy to appreciate why this town was never violated by a beseiging enemy – hence its description as the Virgin of Languedoc. Apart from the secular buildings, the churches of St Michel and St Vincent are notable, with unique sculptures and paintings. *Béziers 78km/48mi, Perpignan 115/71, Toulouse 92/57.*

The walls, Carcassonne

Montpellier H8

Hérault (pop. 196,000) Montpellier, a university town and capital of Languedoc, was originally owned by the Counts of Toulouse and was later a dominion of Sardinia. It did not become French until 1349. A centre of Protestantism, it suffered a terrible siege for eight months in 1622 at the hands of Louis XIII. The town has many narrow, steep streets bordered by fine medieval and 18th-century houses. A triumphal arch stands in the terraced Promenade du Peyrou with its imposing fountains. The university's botanical gardens have existed for four centuries.

42km/26mi north of the town, on the D986, is the **Grotte des Demoiselles**, a series of caves of unsurpassed beauty and size which local peasants believed to be the secret land of the fairies. The largest cave, with weird stalactites giving the impression of human forms and decorations, is like a natural cathedral, with a roof as high as that of Westminster Abbey. *Nimes 52km/32mi.*

Narbonne K5

Aude (pop. 40,000) Narbonne is now well inland, but when the Romans developed it, the salt water lagoons were deep and tidal, and the town was a larger port than Marseille. The incomplete cathedral of St Just (13th-century) was intended to emulate Amiens, and the arch of the choir is a towering Gothic masterpiece – which is as far as money and ingenuity permitted the 13th-century builders to proceed. *Spanish frontier through Perpignan 90km/56mi.*

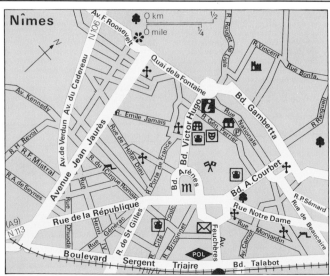

Nîmes   G9

Gard (pop. 134,000) Nîmes is the oldest
Roman city in France. The amphitheatre
had seats for 20,000. In the Middle Ages
the entire population lived inside its walls.
The Maison Carrée, now used as a
museum housing the Venus of Nîmes
among wonderful specimens of Roman
art, was erected as a memorial to the
grandsons of Augustus. The building ap-
pealed so much to Louis XIV that he
wanted to remove it to Versailles. Other
Roman relics are the Temple of Diana,
baths and a gate. The Fountain Gardens
(18th-century) are regarded as among the
loveliest in France. 20km/12mi east on
N106 is the **Pont du Gard**, a water bridge
built by Agrippa in the 1st century BC to
supply water to Nîmes. It has three rows
of arches, one above the other, and is a
unique Roman monument. *Aix-en-
Provence 106km/66mi, Lyon 250/155.*

Perpignan   M4

Pyr-Orientales (pop. 108,000) Perpignan
was once the capital of the independent
kingdom of Mallorca. The huge citadel
contains the palace of the 13th-century
kings. The 14th-century red brick castle is
now an arts and crafts museum. Very
Spanish in character, the town has some
notable festivals, particularly at Easter.
For visitors wanting to see the district,
and for tourists going to Spain, information and permits, *etc*, are available at the
Tourist Bureau, Quai de-Lattre-de-
Tassigny. *Spanish frontier 25km/16mi.*

Villeneuve-lès-Avignon   G10

Gard (pop. 10,000) This town is often
merely noticed across the river from the
papal palace at Avignon, but can in fact
excel the latter in artistic treasures. Its
situation on the right bank of the Rhône
made it important for the defence of the
south west. At the end of the graceful St
Bénézet Bridge is the 14th-century
Philippe Tower; the St André Fort is one
of the best preserved medieval strongpoints in the country. When the Pope
moved to Avignon, Villeneuve became a
residential area for the princes of the
church: several cardinals' mansions
remain almost perfectly preserved. The
collegiate church of Notre Dame (14th-
century) has a priceless ivory statue of the
Virgin; the Charterhouse, founded by
Pope Innocent VI (whose tomb is in the
hospice chapel), includes cloisters, the
Pope's private chapel and a small church.
In the hospice is one of the world's great
masterpieces: Charenton's *Coronation of
the Virgin. Orange 22km/14mi.*

The Amphitheatre, Nîmes

PROVENCE AND THE CÔTE D'AZUR

For most of the year the visitor will know when he is entering Provence. There is something about the light, even on those rare overcast days of early winter, which is unique, as scores of major artists have appreciated.

It is a large region, geographically divided into three contrasting areas. In the north are the lofty peaks of the Alps with awe-inspiring views, tiny villages, serene lakes and a few small towns which seem to have ignored time itself. A more familiar view of this sun-soaked land emerges as one travels south. The mountain slopes to the east are more gentle, and around the Rhône the countryside is lush and fertile even when the heat paints the rest of the landscape golden-bronze.

Then comes the first glimpse of the azure blue of the Mediterranean. Stretching from Menton to St-Raphaël, the Côte d'Azur was the world's first coastal playground, at the outset for the almost exclusive enjoyment of the wealthy. The entire coast is protected on the north and north east by mountains, so that more than three nights of frost a year are virtually unknown. This rather precise definition of the Côte d'Azur is jealously guarded, but in reality, except in brief periods of wintry gales, the coast further west is just as attractive, and the visitor will note little difference in climate. Indeed, from the historical viewpoint it is more interesting, for this zone was preferred by the Roman conquerors and every town, large or small, is a record in stone of two thousand years and more. Inland are vineyards, quiet forests and vast stretches of low-lying hills covered with scrub, gorse and flowers, both wild and cultivated. Like its luxurious neighbour to the east, the zone near the sea is crammed with resorts, hotels and camping sites wherever there is a little beach. But life is simpler, cheaper and perhaps more restful than in the fashionable places such as Monte Carlo, Nice and Cannes.

Bouillabaisse and Rosé With the exception of Paris, the hotels and restaurants along the coast serve the best and most varied dishes in the country – expensive, generous in quantity and unsurpassed in quality. The chefs are fortunate in having on the doorstep fresh supplies the year round of fruit, vegetables, fish and meat.

Despite the cosmopolitan trends, traditional Provençal dishes maintain their place. The best known is *bouillabaisse*, advertised by every other restaurant. For the genuine dish made with a great variety of fish (which must include octopus), flavoured and coloured by saffron, one should choose a restaurant which insists on twenty-four hours' notice of your visit, and the bowl brought to the table will be so large that neither the patron nor his customers will expect to have any other food at the meal except perhaps some fresh fruit.

Other popular dishes include *bourride* (a simpler version of bouillabaisse) and *brandade* (cod baked in olive oil).

For a light meal when the weather is hot some fresh bread, butter and *salade niçoise* will hurt neither one's purse nor digestion. The salad consists of generous portions of green peppers, aubergines, tomatoes, green beans, olives and anchovies. If you prefer something cooked *ratatouille* is good – aubergines, courgettes, peppers, and tomatoes just tenderized in olive oil.

Pizzas are on sale at serve-yourself restaurants, and usually include anchovies. A similar snack dish is *pissaladière* (olives, anchovies and onions on a coarse bread). Meat dishes which are a Provençal speciality include a beef stew with plenty of vegetables, roast mutton from sheep grazing on the aromatic plants in the Alps, and Arles sausages.

From the strawberries of May to the figs of autumn, masses of fruit are always available, invariably served fresh, *au naturel*. There are some good Alpine cheeses, notably a blue one with a mild flavour.

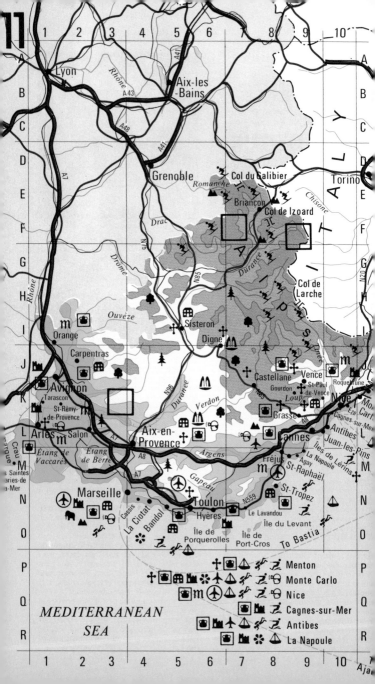

Provençal wines are not well known outside France, but are good and inexpensive. Try Belet and Villars or any of the rosé wines.

Festivals and Events January, car rally Monte Carlo. Pre-Lent (12 days around Shrove Tuesday), 'King of the World' carnival – Nice. February (mid-month), mimosa festival – Cannes. February (last week), lemon festival – Menton. February to March), opera season – Monte Carlo. February (last two weeks), international TV festival – Monte Carlo. March (first two weeks), international trade fair – Nice. Eastertide, international tennis tournament – Monte Carlo. April (last part), international TV programme fair – Cannes. May (last week), international Grand Prix – Monte Carlo. May, international film festival – Cannes. May (mid-month), rose festival – Grasse. May (last two weeks), marine and exploration film festival – Toulon. May 16–18, processions – St-Tropez. June to mid-July, classical music festival – Toulon. June (third Sunday), gorse festival – Roquebrune. June (last Sunday), Festival of the Tarasque – Tarascon. July–August, drama and music festival – Aix-en-Provence. July, jazz festival – Antibes. July-August, drama festival – Orange. July, music festival – Avignon. July (mid-month), mountaineering festival – Briançon. July 29, second part of Tarasque festival – Tarascon. August 1, 500-year-old religious processions – Roquebrune. August, chamber music festival – Menton. August (last week), lavender fair – Digne. September, traditional fair – Tarascon. October (Sunday nearest to October 22), pilgrimage – Les Stes-Maries-de-la-Mer. December 20, Christmas Pastorale – Toulon. December 24, street processions of pilgrims – Menton.

Agay   M9

Var (pop. 1000) Well sheltered by the Estérel mountains, this small resort, with coves and rocky headlands covered with shrubs and flowers, is popular with campers and travellers. There is a pretty harbour bordered by beaches of red sand. *Cannes 30km/19mi.*

Aix-en-Provence   L4

Bouches-du-Rhône (pop. 114,000) Aix-en-Provence is a restful, beautiful town whose descriptive name 'City of Fountains' is amply justified by the water which cascades in a score of squares, along the tree-shaded main thoroughfare and more ornately in the Place Gén.-de-Gaulle outside the municipal centre. The Romans settled here because of the warm and medicinal springs, and it is still a popular spa, treating circulatory and

blood diseases. Its most notable buildings are 17th- or 18th-century, including the Hôtel de Ville and the bishop's palace. The cathedral of St Sauveur (6th to 16th century) has fine tapestries and famous carved, folding doors. Among the many museums the tapestry collection behind the cathedral is unique. The Musée Granet, in rue Cardinale, has the finest collection of French art outside the Palais du Louvre. This was the town where Cézanne lived and painted. Aix's festival of the arts (July–August) is of world-wide importance. *Marseille 30km/19mi.*

Antibes   L10

Alpes-Maritimes (pop. 56,000) Antibes is at least 2500 years old. The Greeks ejected the local fishermen and built their own port and mercantile centre on this promontory of low rocks. The Romans, Saracens, English and Austrians have all in their turn attacked it and sometimes taken over its fortress. The area of Antibes has the most equable climate in Provence. Hence it is a centre for the cut flower industry, with acres of carnations, roses and orchids almost always in bloom. The town is the ideal centre from which to visit the inland towns and villages – **Biot**, with its gay little museum devoted to the works of Fernand Léger; and **Cros-de-Cagnes**, where Renoir lived.

Arles   L1

Bouches-du-Rhône (pop. 50,000) Like its venerable sister-town of Nîmes, Arles begs the tourist to deviate from the direct routes to the Côte d'Azur and take the N570 or N113. Here is a Roman town more vividly conveying one back to the pre-Christian era than is possible even in Rome. The great arena, with seats for 25,000, is older than the Colosseum. Founded by Julius Caesar, Arles became the second city of the Roman Empire under Constantine. Particularly fascinating are the underground storehouses, cool and dry, where grain and wine were kept and markets were held. Baths, a cemetery (*Alyscamps*), an obelisk and roads are other Roman features. The cloisters of St Trophime are a beautiful example of 12th-century architecture.

South east of Arles lies the barren land known as the **Crau**. The legend is that the pebbles were scattered here by the gods to aid Hercules in his battle with the Ligurians. Beyond it is **Salon**, where the famous seer Nostradamus lived and is buried. South west is the **Camargue**, bounded by two branches of the Rhône. One area is a vast bird sanctuary with thousands of aquatic birds, including flamingoes, egrets and ibis. The herds of semiwild cattle and wild white horses are carefully preserved, watched over by horsemen who gave the skills of the cowboy to America. Part of the Camargue has been developed by irrigation and draining, so that the salt marshes of a few years ago have become 12,500 hectares/30,000 acres of rice fields. A complete inspection of this wild and primitive area is possible only on horseback; tours are organized at Arles. Permission to visit the protected zones is given only to accredited naturalists and research workers after application to the Directeur de la Reserve Nationale, 1 rue Stendhal, 13200 Arles. *Marseille 90km/56mi, Nîmes 31/19.*

Camargue horses

Avignon   J1

Vaucluse (pop. 93,000) Avignon, the gateway of Provence, stands near the junction of the Rhône and Durance. Though a flourishing modern city, the centre is still enclosed by ramparts pierced by numerous gates. Avignon is famous as the home of the Popes during the 'Babylonian captivity' (1309–77). The papal palace, a vast, rambling building which is a mixture of fortress and luxurious residence, stands on a hill overlooking the river. Many of the furnishings and artistic treasures were destroyed or pillaged during the French Revolution. Some of the smaller rooms, notably the papal bedchamber and those in the wardrobe tower, still provide the tourist with a picture of the medieval splendour. Many relics of the palace, retrieved after the Revolution, are housed in the excellent Musée Calvet adjacent to the palace. The famous bridge immortalized in the children's song is best seen from the palace gardens, high above the river. *Marseille 100km/62mi.*

Bandol   N5

Var (pop. 7000) A largely unspoiled fishing port and the centre of the wine-growing area of Provence. The beaches, well-protected by wooded hills, are of fine sand and the bathing is safe for children. The houses rise in tiers from the coastline beside narrow alleys and steep streets. The botanical gardens with semitropical plants and exotic birds are evidence of the gentle climate the year round. *Toulon 18km/11mi.*

Briançon   E8

Hautes-Alpes (pop. 11,000) Briançon claims to be the highest city in western Europe. It stands nearly 1400m/4600ft above sea level, and from either north or south the motorist climbs at least 600m/1900ft higher to negotiate either the Galibier or Izoard passes. Briançon was developed as a military town by Louis XIV; the ramparts and look-out towers remain. The modern town lies below the walls. In summertime this is a great centre for mountaineers and hikers; in winter for all ice and snow sports; there is a huge skating rink, a bobsleigh run and a ski jump. *Grenoble 116km/72mi.*

Cagnes-sur-Mer   K10

Alpes-Mar (pop. 30,000) Although given the addition of -sur-Mer, the town stands a mile away from the beach and low-lying land with camping and trailer sites. It is a small hill town described by Renoir as the most perfect dwelling place in France. The artist lived here for thirteen years. His garden and studio are maintained as a museum. The 14th-century castle, the residence of the Grimaldi family (rulers of Monaco), was largely rebuilt in the 17th century. From the terraces are fine views of the coast and mountains. *Nice 10km/6mi.*

Cannes   L9

Alpes-Mar (pop. 71,000) Cannes has the reputation of being impossibly expensive. This may be true as regards the luxury hotels on the Croisette, but Cannes is an extensive resort, with an official list of more than 6000 hotel bedrooms, and as many again in the suburbs and nearby villages. A few hundred metres from the harbour or the casino are hotels charging a fraction of the price of those patronized by the millionaires who expect to be seen at Cannes. **Super-Cannes** and **Le Cannet** are not only less expensive; they are quieter, cooler on a summer's night and more truly Provençal than the international establishments in the city centre.

Cannes harbour is the embarkation point for visiting the **Iles de Lérins**. St-Honorat still has a monastery (open to male visitors). Here St Patrick reputedly received his religious education. Ste Marguérite, named after the sister of St Honorat, who founded the monastery, is the alleged place where the man in the iron mask was imprisoned. Dumas' story is fictional, but tourists are obligingly shown the cell where the prisoner lived for so many years. *Aix-en-Provence 160km/99mi, Nice 34/21.*

Avignon

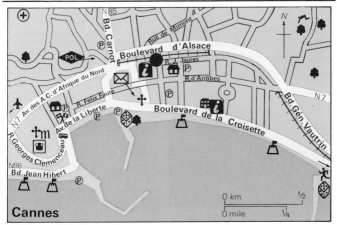

Cannes

Carpentras   J2

Vaucluse (pop. 25,000) This town was originally the capital of a large area in the possession of the Pope. The only relic of the 14th-century fortifications is the Orange Gate. The cathedral is of historical interest because it was begun by the 'anti-Pope' Benedict XIV in the 15th century. The interior presents an almost bewildering array of flamboyant and rich decorations. Nearby the 18th-century Hôtel de Ville has a splendid staircase, chapel and a chamber originally used as a pharmacy. A most unusual establishment in a Provençal town is the 18th-century synagogue, full of beautiful craft work in wrought iron and wood. *Digne 140km/ 87mi, Marseille 115/71.*

Cassis   N4

Bouches-du-Rhône (pop. 6000) Cassis, 19km/12mi from Marseille, is a popular weekend resort for the people of that town. The view as one approaches on the D559 is breathtaking: just before the steep descent to the village the huge bay of Marseille comes into view. Cassis is a small port; the beach is mainly pebbles. The great attraction is the Calanques, the scores of creeks to the west of the three beaches which honeycomb the cliffs, some of which tower 180m/590ft above them. *Toulon 44km/27mi.*

Castellane   K7

Alpes-de-H-Prov (pop. 1200) Castellane, well known as a resting place on the N85 from Cannes to the north, is a pretty little Alpine town with medieval streets and an 11th-century church. 16km/10mi south, on the D952 is the Grand Canyon of the **Verdon**, a gorge in places over 1000m/ 3300ft deep. *Cannes 80km/50mi.*

La Ciotat   N4

Bouches-du-Rhône (pop. 33,000) La Ciotat, a resort with modern dockyards well away from the old port, stands on a magnificent bay with 6km/4mi of beach. At the eastern end are the peaceful resorts of **Les Lecques** and **St-Cyr**. They stand on the site of a prehistoric port taken over by the Romans for an attack on Marseille. 24km/15mi inland is the lonely grotto of **Ste Baume**, where tradition has it that Mary Magdalene lived and expiated her sins. Midnight mass is celebrated in her cave on 22 July each year. *Marseille 34km/21mi.*

Digne   I6

Alpes-de-H-Prov (pop. 17,000) A quiet town, Digne marks the start of the mountainous stretch for the motorist driving south. The large church, regarded as one of the best examples of the Romanesque style in France, once ranked as a cathedral. The springs in this area from the limestone are regarded as medicinally valuable for treating skin and rheumatic diseases. *Avignon 142km/89mi.*

Eze   K10

Alpes-Mar (pop. 1800) Eze is a fantastic example of the almost unapproachable site the inhabitants of Provence had to choose in the times when pirates and Moors regularly attacked them. The village is perched precariously around a pointed mass of rock 400m/1300ft above the sea. There is no road traffic in the village, approachable by a footpath from the coast. The Upper Corniche road from Nice to Menton enables one to look down on the village, the Middle Corniche is provided with ample parking space near the village and the coastal Corniche runs through the modern little resort of **Eze-sur-Mer**, which has a narrow beach. There is a steep climb from the coastal Corniche to Eze. *Nice 11km/7mi.*

Eze-sur-Mer, from Eze

Fréjus   M8

Var (pop. 31,000) The name is a contraction of *Forum Julii*, after Julius Caesar who constructed a harbour, storage buildings and forts as a centre where troops from Rome were disembarked and provisioned for the control of Gaul. Here Agricola, conqueror of Britain, was born. Much of the Roman town has been covered by later buildings or by the silting of the River Argens, but just outside the town are several sections of an aqueduct. Fréjus was partially damaged by a tragic dam burst above the town, though its own position above river and sea level left the centre unharmed.

Immediately east of the town is **St-Raphaël**, a modern resort with good sands, which is regarded as the gateway to the French Riviera. The inland roads to Nice cut through the wooded hills to Cannes en route. The coast road winds along the edge of the **Estérel**, a wild and lovely stretch of hills and mountains, covered with undergrowth whose name has gone into history: *Maquis*, the name for the French underground fighters of the Second World War. A dozen tiny resorts, camping sites and holiday villages nestle in the coves and bays of this stretch of coast as far as **La Napoule** on the edge of Cannes. *Cannes 35km/22mi.*

Grasse   L9

Alpes-Mar (pop. 35,000) Grasse is the town that the discerning tourist in search of both peace and economy often selects for his stay on the Riviera. It lies 16km/10mi from Cannes on the slopes of the mountains. It is the world's scent centre, and the gentle breezes which keep the temperature equable are always redo-

lent of flowers. The various perfume distilleries welcome visitors on conducted tours at frequent intervals each day. All around the town are immense flower fields annually producing vast quantities of orange blossom and rose petals. This was the town where Fragonard lived. The museum contains relics of his life and many of his works.

North of Grasse are the **Gorges du Loup**, a wild and picturesque area of ravines, cascades and villages built on the top of steep hills, notably **Gourdon**. The restaurants dotted around this district are famous for trout taken straight from the pools and streams. *Cannes 16km/10mi.*

Hyères   N6

Var (pop. 42,000) This is one of the oldest coastal resorts in Provence, 'discovered' by the English a century ago because of its perfect winter climate, the hills protecting it from the Mistral, the wind which occasionally howls from the land mass behind the coast. In fact the English knew Hyères long before, because this was an embarkation point for the Crusades. The sea has receded, leaving the old town a mile or two inland, and a suburb, Giens, has grown beside the sea.

Seawards are the Îles d'Or, so called from the golden hue of the mica-flecked rocks in sunlight. Largest of the three islands is **Île de Porquerolles**, state-owned; there are some hotels and cafés. **Île de Port-Cros**, densely covered with lush vegetation, is a nature reserve. Camping, lighting fires, even smoking are forbidden. **Île du Levant** has a nudist colony; a large area of the island is a prohibited defence zone of the French Navy. Boats for the islands leave from Cavalaire, Giens, Hyères, Le Lavandou, Toulon. *Cannes 126km/78mi, Toulon 20/12.*

Juan-les-Pins   L9

Alpes-Mar Juan-les-Pins was one of the first Riviera resorts to be developed when the cult of sunbathing arrived between the two world wars. It is a smart and expensive resort, with a casino, night clubs cabarets and a splendid sandy beach which includes a café where drinks are served on floating trays in the water. The bay is a great centre for waterskiing.

More attractive for those of moderate means is neighbouring **Golfe-Juan**, a pretty little resort midway between Cannes and Juan-les-Pins. There is a small fishing harbour where Napoleon landed when he escaped from Elba; the café where he refreshed himself before his triumphant march to Paris still serves drinks in the main street. On the hill above

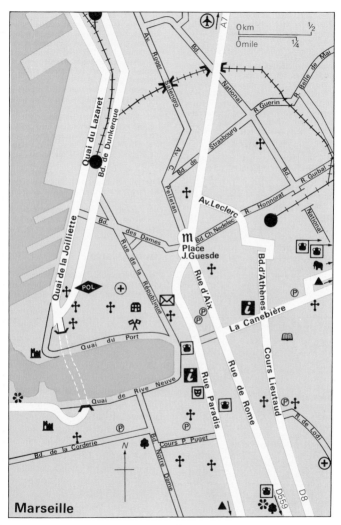

Marseille

Golfe-Juan is the ceramics village of **Vallauris**, where Picasso lived for ten years, making pottery. *Cannes 11km/7mi.*

Le Lavandou N7

Var (pop. 4000) Le Lavandou is one of the fastest growing Mediterranean resorts. What was – and still is – a fishing village has been surrounded by modern hotels, flats, camping sites, and yacht basin, with a casino, night clubs and famous restaurants. The sandy beach, sloping gently into the sea, is some 3km/2mi long and capable of taking innumerable visitors without congestion. Offshore fishing is reputedly the finest on the coast. Behind the town the wooded hills climb abruptly towards the mountains. Periodically serious forest fires break out in this area, so camping, while permitted, is subject to strict controls. 5km/3mi inland is the medieval village, **Bormes les Mimosas**. *Toulon 43km/27mi.*

Marseille   N4

Bouches-du-Rhône (pop. 915,000) Twenty-seven centuries ago the Ionians, fleeing from the Persians, landed on the great bay which is now Marseille (Marseilles), founding the first Greek city of western Europe, long since hidden by successive towns built where the Vieux Port (Old Port) now stands. (Even this is new: the Germans destroyed the area.) From here stretches the Canebière, a street of shops, cafés and amusement places, ending at the Boulevard de la Libération. The pavements are always crowded with visitors from every corner of the world. The city's eight museums cover every facet of art, history and industry. *Lyon 315km/195mi.*

Menton   K11

Alpes-Mar (pop. 25,000) Menton, the last town of the French Riviera before the Italian frontier on the outskirts, is really two communities. The old town, easily missed because of the new road tunnel beneath it, once again enjoys peace and quiet in its narrow streets with fishermen's houses. The newer part is spacious, with shady avenues and hotels of all grades. The beach of white pebbles contrasts vividly with the brilliant blue of the sea. There are several well equipped bathing areas, some with patches of sand. Two important events in Menton are the Festival of Lemons (growing in profusion around the town) in February and the chamber music festival in August. The museum in the rue Lorédan-Larchey has archaeological exhibits and a fine collection of modern paintings, including prize-winning works from the Menton Biennal. Just outside the town, where the Corniche road ends, stands **Roquebrune**, a fortified village with a château originating in the 10th century; Sir Winston Churchill enjoyed many holidays here. 8km/5mi farther up the Grande Corniche is **La Turbie**, a Roman city with the remains of the huge tower Caesar Augustus erected in 6 BC to commemorate his subjection of the Alpine tribes. Seawards from La Turbie is a vantage point from which to look down on Monte Carlo 300m/980ft below. *Nice 29km/18mi.*

Monte Carlo   K11

(Pop. 25,000) Monte Carlo, capital of the independent principality of Monaco, was originally a pirate stronghold. The visitor will be unaware that he is leaving France.

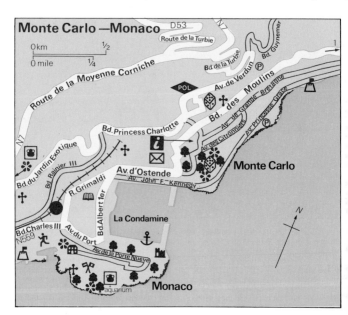

No one demands a passport; no baggage is examined. The fact that the frontier has been crossed is known only by a different name on signpost identification, the police in British-style helmets and perhaps by the sparkling cleanliness everywhere. This community actually consists of four districts: **Monaco**, perched on a rock above the sea with its palace, cathedral, government offices and aquarium; **La Condamine**, the commercial and residential area; **Fontvieille**, with light industries including a glass factory open to visitors; and **Monte Carlo**, gambling centre and luxury resort. Though 34-storey blocks of flats have marred the immaculate beauty of the past, Monte Carlo is still the perfect picture postcard from any viewpoint.

Once the most exclusive playground in the world, it now offers many attractions to the ordinary tourist. All roads lead through palm-shaded avenues to the square with a beautifully kept garden where the casino stands. The so-called private rooms are both expensive and exclusive, but in the public rooms anyone can have a mild flutter on the tables for a few francs, and in the daytime there are no restrictions as regards formal attire. The casino has a tiny theatre which is an architectural masterpiece, a concert hall and bars overlooking the sea. Nearby is the Café de Paris where, before dinner, one can usually see a few celebrities sipping an aperitif. Before leaving this area, full information about hotels, restaurants and places of interest can be obtained from the information bureau at 2 Boulevard des Moulins.

The heart of the town lies 800m/½mi to the south west on a rocky promontory reached through twisting, hilly avenues or along the Avenue de Monte Carlo. The palace, the home of the reigning Grimaldi family, is a charming building guarded by men in toy soldier costume. (The changing of the guard ceremony takes place at midday.) Conducted tours of the ballroom, throne room and chapel take place at frequent intervals throughout the day, even if the members of the family are in residence. The promontory has several centres of interest – the cathedral, the Hôtel de Ville and the parliamentary buildings, and, perched on the cliffs, the oceanographic museum. This includes the world's largest aquarium. The museum is a memorial to the work of Prince Albert I, who died in 1925. He was one of the world's greatest marine biologists. A final visit should be made to the exotic gardens, ingeniously laid out on a rocky hillside. The gardens contain a unique collection of cacti and succulents.

Monaco is for the most part high above the sea. Its natural beaches are narrow and pebbly. At great cost tons of sand have been spread in some areas to provide exclusive sun and sea bathing areas. The largest artificial beach reached along the Avenue Princesse Grace is actually in French territory. New beaches and sun terraces have been built in the central area between the palace and the casino. *Nice 18km/11mi.*

La Napoule   M9
Alpes-Mar La Napoule stands on a long sandy gulf stretching towards Cannes, and has a new yacht marina. The 14th-century castle overlooking the village was restored by the American sculptor, Henry Clews, who also created a garden full of decorative fountains. *Cannes 10km/6mi.*

Nice   K10
Alpes-Mar (pop. 350,000) Nice was a village in 350 BC – and probably a tribal centre long before that because prehistoric sites are still being uncovered in the vicinity. The old town around the harbour is a network of narrow streets and wide cool squares, many with large open air markets for fruit, vegetables and flowers. The area is dominated by a pine-covered hill, the Rocher du Château, which until the 18th century provided the town's defences. The hill is now a restful place on which to relax and enjoy the views over miles of coast. The modern town is spread along the beach of the Baie des Anges, with the famous Promenade des Anglais, a wide thoroughfare of palm trees, roses and flower beds, extending for more than 6km/4mi to the runways of Nice airport.

The town is rich in museums and art galleries. The Musée Masséna (35 Promenade des Anglais) has the appearance of an 18th-century palace; it was actually built in 1900. There are magnificently furnished rooms and paintings by the Impressionists. The Musée des Beaux Arts (Avenue des Baumettes) contains Gobelin tapestries, ancient and modern paintings, and oriental sculpture. A new museum off Avenue George V is devoted entirely to works by Marc Chagall. For the tourist perhaps the most fascinating museum is at 59 Avenue St Barthélémy. The building is an ancient farmhouse which has been meticulously reconstructed as a 15th-century priory.

In the residential district of **Cimiez** long-term excavations are revealing remains of Greek and Roman occupation: a temple, baths and private villas. Facing these is the Musée Matisse, an 18th-century mansion in which the works of the artist, who lived most of his life in the town, are on display.

Nice is, of course, world famous for its carnival. This takes place on the Thursday before Shrove Tuesday and lasts for 12 days, culminating in a spectacular fireworks display when King Carnival is burned on a large pyre. *Paris 940km/584mi.*

Orange   I1

Vaucluse (pop. 26,000) No traveller approaching by the N7 can have any doubt that this is a Roman city. The first thing seen when coming from the north is the triumphal arch erected by Tiberius, standing in the centre of the road. In the town the road curves round the Roman theatre, which Louis XIV called 'the most beautiful wall in my kingdom'. Wall is an understatement. This is an almost perfectly preserved Roman theatre on a large scale, and it is still used for concerts, operas and plays, with an annual festival in the first ten days of August, when this acoustically perfect arena seating 10,000 echoes to the words of Shakespeare or

Molière just as, 2000 years ago, the Roman colonists enjoyed Euripides and Aeschylus. *Avignon 24km/15mi.*

St-Paul-de-Vence   K9

Alpes-Mar (pop. 2000) St-Paul-de-Vence is a fortified town with a fine Gothic church within the ramparts. The building contains many notable treasures and works of art, including a famous Black Virgin. The Maeght Foundation has unique displays of 20th-century art. In the square is a fountain; legend has it that anyone who drinks from it will not die before he returns to drink again. *Nice 24km/15mi.*

St-Rémy-de-Provence   K1

Bouches-du-Rhône (pop. 9000) This town was not on the itineraries of many tourists in the past but it is an attraction rivalling neighbouring Nîmes. Recent excavations 1½km/1mi south have revealed buildings used by the Greeks in the 2nd century BC and a town of Gallo-Roman origin of the

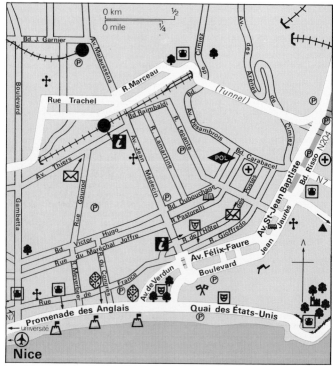

st century AD. Complete streets have been uncovered. A triumphal arch has lost he top part, but the remainder has a vivid bas-relief of chained prisoners; nearby is a mausoleum erected in honour of the grandsons of Caesar Augustus, the only memorial of its kind which has survived. 3km/2mi east is the priory of **St Paul de Mausole**, once a mental home where Van Gogh painted many of his masterpieces. *Marseille 92km/57mi.*

St-Tropez N8

Var (pop. 6000) St-Tropez nestles on the south-western side of the huge Gulf of St-Tropez. Made famous in the late 1950s by film stars and artists, it has now lost some of its fashionable and novelty appeal, which is perhaps a good thing, for it could revert to its place as one of the most charming resorts of the Riviera. It has a long history. Originally a Greek trading port, it was given its new name when Nero, having executed the Christian Torpetius at Pisa, put the corpse in a boat with a cock and a dog to feed on it. The boat, legend tells, drifted ashore months later, with the body untouched and uncorrupted. The fishermen thereupon named their collection of huts St-Torpes. The event is celebrated for three days in mid-May in the *Bravade*, when a replica of the corpse is carried round the town in a boat amid salvoes of firearms.

St-Tropez should at least be visited, though accommodation in the season can be expensive and difficult to find. Many visitors stay on the other side of the gulf at **Ste-Maxime**, where there are many hotels and large camping sites. *Cannes 66km/41mi, Toulon 70/43.*

Sisteron I5

Alpes-de-H-Prov (pop. 7000) The dominant position of this town, towering above the River Durance and the surrounding rocky landscape, marks it as a strong point on the borders of Provence and the Dauphiné, held and attacked for century after century – from Roman times until the Second World War. Steep alleys and winding streets, often passing under houses and through rock, eventually lead to the Romanesque cathedral and the massive citadel, the latter constantly enlarged and strengthened in the 16th to the 18th centuries. It is now used as an open air theatre in the summer for concerts, plays and pageants. *Digne 40km/25mi, Grenoble 140/87.*

Tarascon K1

Bouches-du-Rhône (pop. 11,000) Tarascon, on the left bank of the Rhône, is dominated by the massive fortress completed in the 15th century by the 'Good King René' of Provence. The buildings are in a fine state of repair, with unusual decorative sculptures still bearing traces of their colouring. The church, 12th-century, has been considerably restored. It is dedicated to St Martha, who according to legend destroyed a terrible dragon which was ravaging the countryside. The event is celebrated on the last Sunday in June and in July. *Avignon 24km/15mi.*

Toulon N5

Var (pop. 185,000) Toulon, France's principal naval base, was sorely damaged during the war. The famous Cronstadt Quay has been largely rebuilt, and serves the visitor wanting a pleasant place to stroll and take a drink, as well as the needs of warships and their crews. Much of the old town escaped damage, and the 18th-century streets and houses offer a pleasant contrast to the bustling main street with its department stores and places of entertainment. *Marseille 64km/40mi.*

Vence K9

Alpes-Mar (pop. 12,000) Vence is a centre of farms producing blooms for the Grasse perfumeries. The town was once a bishopric and the cathedral (15th-century) is notable for its magnificent choir stalls. Today's great object of interest is the Dominican chapel decorated by Matisse in 1950 – a small building in brilliant white with black outlines, contrasting with the rich colours of the stained glass; it is regarded as a 20th century masterpiece of religious art (visits restricted: only on currently advertised days and times) *Nice 24km/15mi.*

Vence

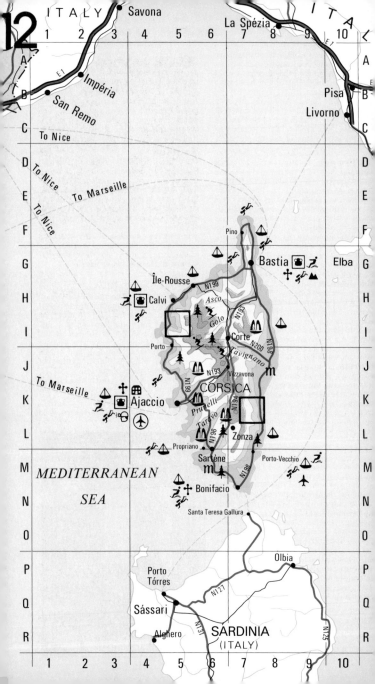

ITALY

Savona

La Spézia

ITALY

1 2 3 4 5 6 7 8 9 10

A

Impéria

Pisa

B

San Remo

Livorno

C

To Nice

D

To Nice

E

To Marseille

To Nice

F

Pino

Bastia

Elba

G

Île-Rousse

N199

H

Calvi

Asco

I

Golo

Corte

N200

N198

Porto

Tavignano

J

N199

N193

Vizzavona

CORSICA

K

To Marseille

Ajaccio

N194

Prunelli

L

Taravo

Zonza

N196

N198

Propriano

Sartène

Porto-Vecchio

M

MEDITERRANEAN

Bonifacio

N

SEA

Santa Teresa Gallura

O

P

Olbia

Porto
Tórres

N127

Q

Sássari

N131

N125

R

Alghero

SARDINIA
(ITALY)

1 2 3 4 5 6 7 8 9 10

CORSICA

Although the island is closer to Italy than France, Corsica is wholly French and administered as a province. Its great appeal, however, is its 'difference' – the highly individual people, their unique customs and way of life. The scenery is awesome in its primitive beauty with vast areas devoid of any sign of human occupation.

While the new hotels and the larger towns are now providing the usual facilities for holiday makers, the visitor should not expect to find much sophisticated entertainment during his stay. Corsica is essentially a place for the lover of the outdoors and of peace and quiet.

For an island the variety of terrain is remarkable. About half of the land is covered with trees and *maquis* (heather, shrubs and myrtle). Mountains rise above these areas to nearly 2700m/9000ft and there is no place where one is not within walking distance of rocky land rising 600m/2000ft behind the serrated coastline.

Although the roads are maintained to the usual Route Nationale standards, they inevitably twist and turn with innumerable steep gradients and 40kph/25mph is regarded as a maximum speed. While without doubt the best way to see Corsica is by using the excellent bus services combined with a couple of hours' walking, no one should miss some travel on the trains which run between Ajaccio, Bastia and Calvi on a breathtaking scenic route reminiscent of the railways in the Swiss Alps.

Smoked pork and Cedratine Dishes unknown on the mainland can make meals in Corsica memorable, not least because so many foods are cooked over fragrant wood embers. Pork from animals fed on chestnuts and smoked slowly over aromatic twigs is an example. Smoked ham and smoked sausages (hot and cold) are also excellent, and tasty for picnics.

Perhaps not surprisingly a splendid variety of fish dishes is available, including a *bouillabaisse* different from that made famous in Provence. Trout from the mountain streams are served within half an hour of being caught.

Chestnuts are used in both savoury and sweet dishes – the latter including chestnut fritters. Visitors may be surprised to see the local people eating a dish of fresh fruit with occasional bites of cheese. The cheese is called Brocciu; it is also used in omelettes and tarts.

There are good white, red and rosé wines. Perhaps unexpectedly, the white wines are stronger than the others, and should be drunk with some caution by those believing white means light.

A tough people who pit their strength against the sea and the harsh life in the mountains need good spirits to keep warm in winter and to relax on a summer evening. Cedratine, made from lemons, is delightful. Myrte, distilled from myrtle berries, has an unforgettable flavour, but is an acquired taste.

Festivals and Events Shrove Tuesday, Mardi Gras festival – Corte. March 18, celebrations in honour of Our Lady of Mercy – Ajaccio. Eastertide, Holy Thursday 'cake' procession – Calvi; Good Friday night processions – Ajaccio, Bastia, Bonifacio, Calvi, Sartène. June 2, St Erasmus procession – Ajaccio. July (last week till mid-August), arts and drama festival – Ajaccio. August 15, celebrations on anniversary of Napoleon's birthday – Ajaccio. September 8–10, festival commemorating nativity of the Virgin – Ajaccio. November (first two weeks), international car rally – Ajaccio/Bastia (alternate years).

Inland from Ajaccio

Ajaccio   K5
Corse du Sud (pop. 52,000) The capital of
Corsica, founded by the Genoese in the
15th century, stands on a bay with mountains around it. The birthplace of
Napoleon, his family home remains as he
knew it. The Hôtel de Ville and cathedral
contain many relics of France's hero.

Bastia   G7
Haute Corse (pop. 52,000) Bastia has
charming Italian-style houses and streets
around the old fishing port. The Genoese
Governor's palace (now a museum) and
the town's many baroque churches are
noteworthy.

Bonifacio   N7
Corse du Sud (pop. 3000) A small community founded as the domain of a Count
of Tuscany in the 9th century, Bonifacio
retains its medieval appearance, still isolated from the rest of the island by a
drawbridge and massive wooden gates.
For its size, the town is incredibly rich in
churches, convents and monuments to its
notable townsfolk over the centuries.

Calvi   H5
Haute Corse (pop. 4000) Calvi is possibly
the most attractive of all the towns for a
seaside holiday with varied activities. It
stands behind massive ramparts on a
promontory overlooking a wide bay, and
has a shipping and yachting harbour. On
one side of the town is a sandy beach
fringed by pinewoods; on the other, rocks
dropping sheer to deep inlets and coves.

Porto-Vecchio   M7
Corse du Sud (pop. 8000) Porto-Vecchio is
yet another fortified town. It nestles in a
long, narrow bay, and behind it the land
rises steadily through dense woods of cork
oaks (the town's major industry) to a
plateau of rocks amid mountain peaks.

Propriano   L6
Corse du Sud (pop. 3500) Propriano, a
small village at the head of a picturesque
gulf, is a good centre for visitors wanting
to explore the interior of the island, and
particularly for touring the prehistoric
sites. This area was the stronghold of the
islanders in resisting the invading
Genoese, and inspired Dumas for his
novel *The Corsican Brothers*.

Ajaccio

Bonifacio

All main entries are printed in heavy type. Map references are also printed in heavy type. The map page number precedes the grid reference.